THE JOKE WAS OVER!

Suddenly, at a few minutes after 3:00 p.m. on October 16, the Mets were World Champions. THE YEAR THE METS LOST LAST PLACE traces the fantastic events of this rise to baseball's summit. Beginning with the crucial nine days in mid-July when the Mets subdued the league-leading Cubs and the hapless Montreal Expos, the authors follow the Amazin' Mets through their stunning playoff sweep of the power-hitting Atlanta Braves, to the incredible string of World Series victories over baseball's winningest team, the Baltimore Orioles.

THE YEAR THE METS LOST LAST PLACE is the story of the New Breed, the new Mets, but it is set against the tragicomic history of the club, against the memories of nine straight defeats at the outset of the Mets' first season, against the memories of Marvelous Marv Throneberry and Rod Kanehl and Elio Chacon and Choo Choo Coleman. It is a book for Mets fans and baseball fans, a book for anyone who cheered for David against Goliath!

THIS IS THE STORY OF LOSERS
WHO LEARNED HOW TO WIN!

Other SIGNET Sports Books
You Will Enjoy

The Year the Mets Lost Last Place

By Paul D. Zimmerman
and Dick Schaap

Updated

A Signet Book
Published by The New American Library

Acknowledgments

The authors would like to thank the following people for contributing material to this book:

Jim Brosnan

Andy Carra

Joe Durso

Larry Fox

Joe Gergen

Richard Gutwillig

Steve Jacobson

Bob Kamman

Jack Lang

Norm Miller

John Monteleone

Bill Quinn

Pamela Susskind

George Vecsey

Art Woodard

Dick Young

Vic Ziegel

Contents

Introduction

Nine Crucial Days

The idea seemed ridiculous: A crisis in the life of the New York Mets. It was enough to make anyone familiar with the history of the Mets double up in laughter.

* * *

Sandy Alomar.
Shaun Fitzmaurice.
Joe Grzenda.
Joe Moock.
Al Schmelz.

The names ring out—the names of the men who have worn the uniform of the New York Mets. Misspellable names. Unpronounceable names. Forgettable names, matched to forgettable deeds.

* * *

In the first seven years of their existence, from 1962 through 1968, the New York Mets faced a crisis every day. The crisis was not whether they would win, but whether they would live.

Marvelous Marv Throneberry, who impersonated a first baseman for two seasons, might be skulled by a pop fly. Roger Craig, who lost forty-six games in two years, including eighteen in a row the second year, when he felt at home, might be decapitated by a line drive. Elio Chacon, who could play short, second or third with equal risk, might lose his teeth to a ground ball. And the young Ron Swoboda, the brave bull, might pursue a fly ball and gore either himself or any other outfielder who came too close to his horns.

Never in the history of baseball had so many men played so poorly for so long.

* * *

But by June, 1969, the New York Mets, for seven years the funniest team in all baseball—unlike the old St. Louis Browns, the Mets didn't have to use gimmicks like a pinch-hitting midget to draw laughs; they did it on sheer ineptitude—suddenly were no longer playing comedy. They were playing baseball, good baseball, and when they won their first eight games in June—after closing May with three straight victories—they owned an eleven-game winning streak, the best of their lives, the best in the National League in 1969.

The eleven-game winning streak gave birth to this book: a look at the Mets under pressure. They had charged into second place, but early in July, they were going to face a dangerous test—nine crucial days, ten crucial games. First, on July 8, 9 and 10, they were going to play single games in New York against the Chicago Cubs, the National League leaders. Then, on July 11, 12 and 13, they were going to entertain the Montreal Expos—the expansion team, the 1969 version of the 1962 Mets—for two single games and a doubleheader. And then, on July 14, 15 and 16, they were going to invade Chicago for three single games against the Cubs in Wrigley Field. If they could hold their own over those nine days, the Mets would establish themselves as pennant contenders. But if they were to collapse, no one would be greatly surprised; after all, they had perfect breeding for a collapse.

This book, then, is an examination of the nine crucial days, minute-by-minute, as reported by more than a dozen different persons, most of them New York newspapermen, one an ex-major-league baseball player, Jim Brosnan, who suffered many indignities during his career, but pitching for the Mets was not one of them.

* * *

As the Cub series at Shea Stadium approached, New York City found itself gripped by a vaguely familiar epidemic—baseball fever. Until mid-1969, most people suspected baseball fever was dead in New York, killed by the New York Jets, the New York Rangers and the New York Knicks, all of whom enjoyed exciting seasons in 1968–69, and by the New York Yankees, who didn't.

The most rabid fans in New York baseball history had always been the followers of the New York Giants and the Brooklyn Dodgers, and when the Giants and the Dodgers moved to the West Coast in 1958, their fans were crushed. Many of them simply turned away from baseball; they had always thought of the game as a sport, but the team owners—Walter O'Malley and, to a lesser extent, Horace Stoneham—had convinced them that it was a business. Some of them started going to Yankee Stadium to heckle the Yankees, but the Yankees won so consistently the hecklers realized they were wasting their efforts. And some of them, in 1962, with the birth of the Mets, turned to the new National League team in New York. They enjoyed the Mets; they could cheer and laugh and, every so often, they could see old favorites, like Willie Mays and Don Drysdale, come into New York wearing San Francisco and Los Angeles uniforms. But they didn't go to the ball park to see the Mets win; there were some crazy fans, but they weren't that crazy. They came to accept the fact that, starting on Opening Day, the Mets' season would run downhill.

But if the Mets stumbled through the mid-1960s, the New York Yankees tumbled, first at the box office, then on the field. In 1961, the last year the Yankees had the city to themselves, they drew more than 1,700,000 spectators. In each of the next five years, as the Mets' attendance steadily climbed, the Yankees' attendance declined, down to a post-war low of 1,124,648 in 1966, the year the Yankees—who had won the American League pennant fifteen times between 1947 and 1964—sank into tenth place. The same year, which was the first year the Mets soared out of tenth place and into ninth, the National League New Yorkers drew 1,932,693 fans.

Ever since 1965, when they outdrew the Yankees by half a million spectators, the Mets have been *the* baseball team in New York, and the Yankees have been the other team. But neither the Mets nor the other team was able to inspire the kind of passionate interest in baseball that Frank Gifford and Y. A. Tittle and Joe Namath had inspired in football. Not until July 8, 1969, anyway.

Then, for the first time in at least five years, New Yorkers by the millions were talking baseball. Pilots were announcing scores as their planes approached the runways at LaGuardia and J.F.K. airports. Cab drivers were telling their fares about the strengths of the Mets instead of about the weaknesses of Mayor John Lindsay. Businessmen were giving up long martini lunches to rush to the ball park.

It was, to New Yorkers at least, just like the old World Series days, like the days of Babe Ruth and Mel Ott and Jackie Robinson and Joe DiMaggio and Carl Hubbell and Roy Campanella and Lou Gehrig and Frankie Frisch and Duke Snider. Only now the names were Cleon Jones, Tommie Agee and Tom Seaver—all easy to spell, all easy to pronounce, all easy to remember, all New York Mets.

One

The Day the Mets Became a Contender

TUESDAY
JULY 8, 1969

NATIONAL LEAGUE STANDINGS
Eastern Division

	W	L	PCT.	G.B.
Chicago	52	31	.627	—
New York	45	34	.570	5
St. Louis	40	44	.476	12½
Pittsburgh	38	43	.469	13
Philadelphia	36	43	.456	14
Montreal	26	55	.321	25

For the New York Mets in 1962, the first year of their existence, their finest days were rainouts. By their standards, July 8, 1962, was just a typical day's work. They made three throwing errors in one inning, allowed five unearned runs in one inning, lost to the St. Louis Cardinals by fourteen runs, and permitted a forty-one-year-old man to hit three straight home runs against them. Added to the home run he had stroked against the Mets in his final time at bat the previous day, Stan Musial became the first quadragenarian in baseball history to hit four consecutive home runs.

Still, at the end of the long day, even though their record for the season had slipped to 23–59, a percentage of .280, the Mets were only six games behind the Chicago Cubs—which might have been an encouraging sign, except for the fact that the Cubs themselves were in ninth place in the National League, precisely twenty-five and a half games out of first place.

Not until 1967, the sixth year of their history, did the Mets ever win a game on July 8.

8:00 a.m.

For fifteen years, Joseph Ignac of Elizabeth, New Jersey, has not had a winner. In 1954, he cheered the New York Giants to the world championship, but in 1958, when the Giants and Willie Mays fled to San Francisco, Ignac became a man without a team.

He turned, like thousands of National League fans, to Yankee Stadium, the other league, and he pulled for the Chicago White Sox, the Boston Red Sox, the Cleveland Indians, even the Kansas City Athletics, whichever club happened to be facing the New York Yankees. From 1958 through 1961, as the Yankees won three pennants and two World Series, Ignac discovered that Yankee-hating was an exercise in futility.

Logically, when the New York Mets were born in 1962, Joseph Ignac became a follower of futility.

Ignac is not going to work today. The maintenance crew at the Elizabeth courthouse will have to get along without him, but the Mets will not. A white-haired, sixty-five-year-old bachelor, Ignac is going to Shea Stadium. He slips into a plain brown sports shirt and a pair of drab slacks. His socks peek through rips in the stitching of his battered brown shoes.

Fully six hours before game time, he leaves his home to start the two-hour trip to Shea Stadium, first by bus to Manhattan, then by subway to Flushing Meadow. He is leaving so early to make certain he gets a decent seat for a mid-week afternoon game against the Chicago Cubs. As he heads for the park, Ignac is looking forward for the first time to watching his team fight to become a pennant contender.

9:30 a.m.

Jerry Koosman awakens after a restless night. The twenty-five-year-old left-handed pitcher had tried to get to sleep early, after watching the eleven o'clock news, but the opening game of the Chicago series had kept him awake. Koosman, who has an earned run average of 1.67, the best in the National League, is scheduled to star the first game of the series against Chicago's top pitcher, a strapping black Canadian with the unlikely name of Ferguson Jenkins.

With or without Jenkins, the Chicago lineup is enough to ruin any pitcher's sleep. The first three men—shortstop Don Kessinger, second baseman Glenn Beckert and left fielder Billy Williams—are all hitting around .300. After Williams comes Ron Santo, talkative and talented third baseman who leads the league in runs batted in. Then comes Ernie Banks, the first baseman, even more talkative and, at thirty-eight, almost equally talented, still a wise, dangerous power hitter. Behind Banks comes the catcher, Randy Hundley, also a capable power hitter. Even the pitcher is a threat; early in the year, Jenkins blasted a home run off Tom Seaver, the Mets' best pitcher. There are only two visible soft spots. The center fielder, Don Young, is basically a defensive player, and the right fielder, Jim Hickman, doesn't figure to hurt the Mets with his bat. Hickman has already hurt the Mets enough with his bat; he was one of the original Mets and, in 1962 and 1963, he led the team in its strongest batting department—striking out. In 1965, however, Jim Hickman became the first and, so far, only Met to hit three home runs in one game; after one more season, naturally, the Mets traded him away.

Koosman gets up, walks into his kitchen and stares out the back door of his rented two-family home near LaGuardia Airport, some ten minutes by car from Shea Stadium. He is checking to see which way the wind is blowing. "Left field to right," he says. Koosman is pleased. The wind, at least, is on his side, blowing against the power of Chicago's predominantly righthanded lineup.

9:45 a.m.

Donn Clendenon breakfasts at a luncheonette not far from his sixteenth-floor apartment on West 58th Street in Manhattan. A lean, rangy, powerful first baseman, Clendenon came to the Mets a few weeks ago from Montreal in exchange for a handful of young players. In their formative years, the Mets picked up older players, like Duke Snider and Warren Spahn and Ken Boyer, mostly in the hope of luring people to Shea Stadium to watch the past perform. But the trade for the thirty-three-year-old Clendenon was different. He could actually help a club that might have a shot at winning its division. And, in his short stay with the Mets, Clendenon has already made the trade look good. Two days ago, his home run over the right-field screen in Pittsburgh's Forbes Field helped the Mets overcome a four-run Pirate lead and win their fifth straight game.

Nobody recognizes Clendenon or bothers him for autographs as he eats his breakfast. He is still new to New York. He has no complaints about his anonymity. "When people start knowing me here," he says, "I'll find another place to eat. I don't want people asking for autographs. I want to keep my mind on the pitcher."

9:50 a.m.

The Mets' twenty-three-year-old second baseman, Ken Boswell, puts the finishing touches on a steak he is cooking for himself and his roommate, pitcher Danny Frisella, who has just rejoined the team from its Tidewater, Virginia, farm club. Boswell insists he is relaxed. "Nobody feels pressure here," he says. "We're all too young. It's like fighting for the high school championship."

The steak is ready. Boswell, a Texan, takes it to the table, carves it and serves it for himself and Frisella on paper plates. "When we have company," Boswell says, "we use dishes."

10:00 a.m.

Jerry Koosman, wearing black slacks and a blue sports shirt, walks into his back yard. "It's a beautiful day for a ball game," he says, "just the way I like it—not too hot, not too cool." In his last start, in 90-degree weather in St. Louis, he lost fifteen pounds in eight innings of pitching. In the eighth inning, he also lost his control, a 4–0 lead and a chance to win his sixth game of the season. He walked the bases loaded and his relief pitcher, Ron Taylor, gave up a game-tying home run a few moments later. "After a game like that," says Koosman, as he comes back into his house for a breakfast of eggs and sausage, "I can get a cramp in any part of my body. Even if I just lift up my arm, I feel like I can get a cramp."

For Koosman, most of the early part of the 1969 season was spent in pain. He enjoyed a brilliant rookie year in 1968, winning nineteen games, the most ever won by a Met pitcher, but in 1969, his left arm, his pitching arm, began bothering him during spring training in Florida. In his first start of the season, he was hit hard by the St. Louis Cardinals. In his second start, he was hit hard by the Pittsburgh Pirates. He lost that game, 11–2, and afterward, when reporters asked him what was wrong, he told them wryly, "My trouble is that I'm not getting anyone out."

The trouble, actually, was in a muscle behind the shoulder, and, after winning only one game in April, Koosman did not pitch at all for four weeks. He returned late in May, his shoulder ailment cured, and, immediately, he was effective.

Now, coming into the Cub series, he has permitted only nine earned runs in his last seventy-four innings, an incredibly stingy record. Yet, during that stretch, he has won only four games and lost three, mostly because the Mets have not been scoring runs for him. Koosman is not particularly annoyed by the lack of support. The Mets do not score many runs for anyone. They have only one .300-hitting regular, Cleon Jones, and one .300-hitting part-time outfielder, Art Shamsky. Their lineup is enough to strike courage into the hearts of opposing pitchers.

10:05 a.m.

Joseph Ignac of Elizabeth, New Jersey, walks down the subway steps at Shea Stadium, catching a glimpse of the empty green outfield, and heads toward a general admission gate, where tickets go on sale, for $1.30 each, in two hours. Ignac does not worry about finding a decent seat. He is the first man on line at gate E-4.

11:20 a.m.

Jerry Koosman is ready to leave for Shea Stadium. His wife, Lavonne, herds their twenty-one-month-old son, Michael, and two of the neighbors' children—Lavonne baby-sits each morning—into the Koosmans' Pontiac Bonneville. Koosman has worked out a system so that his wife always fills the tank of their car; the key to the system is a limited amount of driving—mostly to the stadium and back—while the pitcher is at home. "My wife waits till we go on the road," Koosman says. "It makes sense, doesn't it, to have a girl buy the gas? They get better service than a man. For a woman, they wash the windshield and check the battery and everything."

Koosman is a farm boy in New York. He grew up in Appleton, Minnesota, where he learned to play baseball in local beer leagues because his high school wasn't big enough to have a team. He played the outfield, and his brother, Orville, usually pitched. But one day the two brothers collided in the outfield; Orville came up with a broken leg, and Jerry moved into the pitching rotation. He was ready. "I'd been practicing in the top of my father's hay barn," he says.

Red Murff, a Met scout who pitched briefly in the big leagues himself, spotted Koosman in 1964 when the young farmer was pitching for Fort Bliss, Texas, and averaging eighteen strike-outs a game. Murff originally offered Koosman a $1,600 bonus to sign, but when the lefthander held out for more money—some of his army teammates told him he ought to get at least $20,000—Murff kept reducing his offer. Koosman signed, finally, for $1,200. He was a bargain. "I figured," says Koosman, "I'd better sign before I owed them money."

On the way to Shea Stadium, young Michael Koosman climbs all over the car, tugging on his father's right arm, the expendable one. Koosman remains calm, undisturbed by his son's antics. But, as the stadium comes into view, Koosman says quietly, "I've never been so nervous about a game in my life."

12:25 p.m.

Shea Stadium has started to fill with the kids who always come out early to watch batting practice and collect autographs. The batting cage has been wheeled out by the ground crew. Coach Joe Pignatano is hitting grounders to the infield. A second- and third-string catcher with the Dodgers in Brooklyn and Los Angeles, Pignatano spent the twilight of a mediocre career as an extra catcher with the original Mets in 1962. Sal Marchiano, a young sportscaster with CBS, is setting up his camera crew to take pictures of batting practice. Pignatano has not forgotten the early days of the Mets. Worried that a wild throw may kill someone, he persuades Marchiano to move his crew.

The area behind the batting cage is crawling with writers and photographers. "There are more writers here than at Cape Kennedy," says one reporter. Nine hundred miles south, at Cape Kennedy, the Apollo 11 astronauts are one week from blastoff.

"It looks like the World Series," another writer agrees. "Everyone's here."

12:30 p.m.

Howard Cosell, the flamboyant sportscaster for ABC, one of the few television reporters who asks athletes real and difficult questions, finishes an interview with Gil Hodges, the Met manager. Cosell wanders over to the box seats where a group of kids are yelling for Hodges' autograph. He raises his arms high, as if to bless the multitude.

"All right, all right, now listen kids, listen," Cosell intones, in a voice reminiscent of W. C. Fields. "Gil Hodges told me to tell you that right after the game he'll be outside with a ball for each one of you."

Cosell repeats his pronouncement in case anyone in the upper deck has missed it. He has stirred up the kids who are now screaming louder than ever. He acknowledges the screams with a gallant wave.

"I've got to admit it," Cosell says to no one in particular. "I own Shea Stadium. Those kids love me."

12:35 p.m.

Ken Boswell stands in the batting cage. He hits several shots that clear the 396-foot mark in right-center field.

"Beautiful," says Jerry Koosman, waiting for his turn to bat. "Hit two or three of those today." Boswell has hit two home runs all season.

12:37 p.m.

Joe Pignatano has stopped hitting grounders and is chatting with two newspapermen, Phil Pepe of the *New York Daily News* and George Vecsey of the *New York Times*.

"When was your last big game?" asks Vecsey.

"Nineteen fifty-nine," says Pignatano. "The second play-off game against the Braves. I got a base hit, no kidding. Hodges walked. I got a single and Furillo hit one over the middle to win the game. It won the pennant for the Dodgers."

"How come *you* were playing?" asks Pepe. "How come they let *you* hit?"

"Roseboro was out of the game," explains Pignatano, throwing Pepe a dirty look. "The team only had two catchers."

"Who was the pitcher?"

"Bob Rush," says Pignatano. "And after that I only got to play one inning in the World Series."

"So this is your first big game since," says Vecsey.

"Big game? What big game? It's only July 8th. The season is only half over. Geez, you guys make it sound bigger than it is. We've got to win a lot of games. This game isn't any more important than playing Pittsburgh or San Francisco or . . ."

"Yeah, but if you beat 'em," cuts in Pepe, nodding toward the Cubs, "it counts as two wins. One for you, one loss for them."

"Yeah," says Pignatano, "but if they lose to somebody else and we win, it's the same thing."

"But you're not guaranteed them losing unless you beat them."

"Well, that's true. But you still have to win every game. Every game is a big game if you want to think about big games."

"Yeah, yeah, sure," say Pepe.

Pignatano looks at him for a moment. "Ever seen anybody as hardheaded as you?" he says.

12:40 p.m.

Jerry Koosman is taking his final turn in the batting cage. The rest of the Mets turn their eyes away, afraid that Koosman's swing may be catching. He has one hit and nineteen strikeouts in thirty-three official times at bat, but he thinks he is beginning to find his groove. "I've been hitting better," Koosman insists. "Well, actually, better in the last game. The first time up I lined out to the second baseman. The second time I flied out to right field and the third time I flied out to center. That's unusual for me, because I usually strike out." In 1968, Koosman set a major league record for strikeouts by a pitcher.

Satisfied with his batting practice, Koosman walks slowly off the field and through the tunnel leading from the Met dugout to the clubhouse. He stands in front of his locker and removes his soaked sweatshirt—"I perspire more than the normal guy"—and puts on a dry one. Joe Deer, the assistant Met trainer, walks up to him.

"Any time you're ready, Jerry," he says.

Koosman takes his pants off and heads for the trainer's room. The ritual is always the same. Sitting on the trainer's table, he extends his left foot. Deer applies a straight razor to a few hairs on the pitcher's instep. He dips a Q-tip into a bottle of tincture of benzoin and smears it around the instep to protect the skin from the adhesive Deer will wrap there. But, before he puts on the adhesive, Deer applies a square patch of moleskin, a soft rabbit fur, to the side of Koosman's big toe.

"I drag my left foot across the mound when I pitch," says Koosman. "If I don't have all this stuff on it, it gets raw."

Deer wraps a strip of elastic tape around the moleskin patch to fix it in place. Koosman is finished and walks back into the locker room.

Matt Winick, the assistant director of Met public relations, hands Koosman a sheet that carries all of the Chicago statistics for that day. Koosman immediately searches for the figures on Ferguson Jenkins, looking for an edge.

"Three wild pitches for him," says Koosman. "I think I've only got two."

12:45 p.m.

Joe Pignatano keeps talking to George Vecsey and Phil Pepe.

"Gilly drove me to the park," says Pignatano, with a glance toward manager Hodges. "I wouldn't go pick *him* up. Hell no! He drives me every day." Hodges, who alternates driving with Pignatano, pays no attention.

"Do the toll takers recognize you?" Vecsey asks Pignatano.

"What are you talking about? There's no toll takers on the Van Wyck Expressway. The day they start charging tolls I'm getting out of baseball. Sometimes the fans recognize Gilly when we're stuck in traffic. But nobody saw us driving in from Brooklyn today. The traffic was moving too fast."

"Was Hodges nervous?"

"No," says Pignatano. "In fact, Gilly was yawning all the way to the ball park."

"Yawning is a sign of nervousness," says Vecsey, smiling slightly.

"It is," chimes in Pepe.

"That's funny," says Pignatano. "I remember Gilly yawning as long as I've known him."

"That's his outlet," says Vecsey. "He doesn't blow his top very often. So he yawns. I think that's how it works."

"Hmm," says Pignatano. "No kidding?"

12:47 p.m.

Yogi Berra, the most successful manager in the history of the New York Yankees—one season, one pennant and one dismissal—and now in his fifth year as a Met coach, is hitting grounders to the infield. Berra, who once told a crowd that was honoring him, "I want to thank everyone who made this night necessary," has a lingering reputation as a wit, which is largely undeserved. He looks funnier than he talks. Berra also has a lingering reputation as one of the greatest catchers in the history of baseball, which is deserved. He averaged twenty home runs a season over eighteen seasons with the Yankees, and he played in fourteen World Series.

A reporter, whose paper has just shifted him from covering the Yankees to covering the Mets, walks up to Berra and mentions that the Yankees are fascinated by the Met drive—which is stretching things. The Yankees are actually only interested in the Met drive, but it isn't easy to strike up a conversation with Berra.

"Hmmmmph," says Berra.

Yogi thinks for a few seconds. "I guess I'll get to watch most of the doubleheader on television tonight," he says. He means the doubleheader in Baltimore between the Yankees and the Orioles.

"They start at 5:30, right?" Berra says. "We should be done by then."

Inside the Yogi Berra who coaches the Mets lives a Yogi Berra who still manages the Yankees.

12:52 p.m.

The Mets finish batting practice. One by one, they start drifting into the clubhouse. Jerry Koosman sits near his locker. "It was so hot on the last trip," he says, "St. Louis . . . Pittsburgh. This is such a nice day. It would be a damn shame if we didn't win." He gets up, moves across the clubhouse and finally sprawls out on the green clubhouse rug in front of pitcher Don Cardwell's locker. Koosman lies there for forty-five minutes.

12:54 p.m.

Eddie Yost, the third-base coach, sits in front of his locker reading the stock market listings. Yost, nicknamed "The Walking Man" during his long career with the Washington Senators for his ability to draw bases on balls, came to the Mets at the beginning of the 1968 season with Gil Hodges. Yost was a coach with the Senators when Hodges was the manager there. A graduate of NYU, he is, perhaps, the only coach in the league with a master's degree in coaching. His thesis at NYU: "Pitchers' Sore Arms: Their Cause, Treatment and Prevention."

"Ready for the big game?" a reporter asks him.

"Nrmph," answers the short, balding Yost, his eyes still fixed on the newspaper. Finally, he puts it down and turns to Joe Pignatano and Yogi Berra, his fellow coaches.

"This morning," he says, "Mike, my five-year-old, he comes busting into the house with the biggest damn dog you ever saw. A big black one, part Great Dane, part German Shepherd. The dog had a collar but Mike wanted to keep the damn thing. You shoulda seen my wife. I said, 'All right, Mike, we'll give it some meat but after you feed it you gotta let it go.' We can't keep a dog like that. But when I was leaving, I heard the kid asking my wife for a rope. He wanted to tie up the dog so he couldn't get away."

"Give the kid a dog, for crying out loud," says Pignatano. "Poor little kid wants to have a dog."

"You could get him a cat," suggests Berra.

"A dog," insists Pignatano. "Kids gotta have dogs."

"But what am I gonna do when we go to Florida?" asks Yost.

"Same damn thing I do," says Pignatano. "Bring it over to my sister and say, 'Take care of this for me.'"

"Get him a cat," says Berra.

"I don't know about pets," says Yost.

12:57 p.m.

Two young men unfurl the first banner of the day at Shea Stadium. It reads: METS ARE HOT BUT CUBS ARE ON TOP. The two young men—eighteen-year-old Roland Pierre and fifteen-year-old Dennis Larsen—are from Brooklyn, but they both became Cub fans when Leo Durocher became manager of the club in 1966. They cheer for the Cubs, but they work for the Mets. They are wearing blue-and-orange vendors' uniforms.

1:15 p.m.

Ron Santo, the Cub third baseman, spots the Mets' starting line-up posted in the Chicago dugout. He walks over to it, looks it over carefully, then shakes his head.

24

"I know Los Angeles won with pitching," Santo says. "But this is ridiculous."

1:20 p.m.

Outside the Cub dugout, Ernie Banks is humming the Met theme song, "Meet the Mets," occasionally singing his own lyrics. "Beat the Mets, beat the Mets," Banks sings. "Come on out and beat the Mets . . ."

Banks is Mr. Sunshine, smiling as usual. Reporters crowd around him, enjoying his performance. After seventeen years in the big leagues, Banks still loves the pre-game whirl of photographers, reporters, kids pleading for autographs.

"What a beautiful day for baseball," he says, as he does before virtually every game. "New York. The melting pot. The Great White Way. What's going on?"

"The Mets," someone tells him.

"What about 'Oh Calcutta?' " Banks asks, referring to the off-Broadway Kenneth Tynan nudity pageant. "Twenty-five dollars a ticket and you can't get a hold of them."

"Don't tell us that beneath that sunshine smile beats the heart of a dirty old man," says one reporter.

"No, no," answers Banks, smiling. "You can't say that. What will all these kids think?"

Finally, someone asks him about the Mets.

"People used to laugh and laugh at the Mets," says Banks. "But not any more. Now they have a good team. They have good pitching and they play together. People laughed a few years ago, but the Mets play together now."

Banks stops and listens to "The Queen of Melody of Shea Stadium," playing a medley on the Thomas Organ.

"That's Jane Jarvis," says Banks, running his hands over an imaginary keyboard. "I remember her when she played at County Stadium in Milwaukee." He smiles broadly.

A reporter asks him what keeps him so exuberant after seventeen seasons with the Cubs, seventeen years without winning a pennant.

"You have to be happy," says Banks, "and sports does it. What kind of world would this be without sports, without baseball?" He raises his bat like a bayonet. "Why, you'd have people at each other all the time."

1:45 p.m.

The teams have finished their batting and infield practice. The scoreboard flashes the starting lineups. The groundskeepers, in Met orange, are putting the final touches on the infield, drawing the batter's box, grooming the mound. Shea Stadium is filled nearly to the last seat.

Down in the far right-field stands, over the Met bullpen, concessionaire #234 prowls through the aisles, yelling: "Soda, soda, get yer ice cold soda. Get yer soda here."

A ten-year-old boy in a Mets cap gets up from his seat and trails the concessionaire. Concessionaire #234 turns to the youngster, holding out his hand for change.

"Don't yell when the game starts," says the boy gravely, giving him nothing. "I want to concentrate."

1:55 p.m.

Leo Durocher slouches in the Chicago dugout, leaning on an outstretched hand, awaiting the start of the game. Durocher spans the history of post-1925, pre-Met baseball in New York. At twenty-two, he was the regular shortstop for the Yankees, a teammate of Babe Ruth; at thirty-five, he managed the Brooklyn Dodgers to a pennant; at forty-five, he managed the New York Giants to a pennant. Blunt, opinionated, excitable, friend of Frank Sinatra and George Raft, baiter of umpires and creator of Willie Mays, Durocher is now, on the brink of his sixty-third birthday, the enemy in New York, the manager of the Cubs.

When Durocher took over the Cubs in 1966, ten years after his last managerial job in the major leagues, he faced a difficult chore. He had a reputation for being able to manage only a winner, and the Cubs were losers. They had finished eighth the previous season. Durocher looked over his material and announced, "This is not an eighth-place ball club."

He was right. By his own definition, Durocher was a nice guy in 1966. The Cubs finished dead last, tenth in the National League. They were the first team in the history of baseball to finish behind the Mets.

But Durocher did not quit, and he guided the Cubs out of the cellar and into third place in both 1967 and 1968. Now, as his Cubs bid for the team's first pennant in a quarter of a century, Durocher is no longer Mr. Nice Guy. He flatly refuses to talk to any reporters before the game.

1:58 p.m.

Jack Lightcap, the Met announcer, delivers the starting lineups over the public address system. The crowd greets every Met name with wild cheers, every name except that of the starting first baseman, Ed Kranepool.

Kranepool is the only current Met who has been with the team since its maiden season. He was brought up at the end of 1962, only seventeen years old, fresh from James Monroe High School in the Bronx, where he had broken the school's home-run record set by Hank Greenberg.

Kranepool was the heart of what Casey Stengel, the first Met manager, once called "The Youth of America," the mythical Met club that would one day win a pennant. But Kranepool was young only in chronology, not in manner. He ran like an eighty-year-old man catching a commuter train. His modest ability to hit became even more modest with men on base. In 1963, when he was only eighteen, teammates considered him "a young fogey," and a banner at the ballpark asked: IS ED KRANEPOOL OVER THE HILL?

But, every now and then, Kranepool showed flashes of the brilliance that had been expected of him. For a few weeks, usually at the start of the season, he would hit over .300, and Met fans, starved for a hero, would rally to him. But then Kranepool would start slipping toward his own level—his own level, according to his career batting average, is .248—and the fans would abandon him. Rumors persisted that Kranepool's attitude was not ideal, that he could have worked harder to break his slumps. The harsher fans called him lazy.

This season, although he has already driven in thirty-one runs, ten more than he did in all of 1968, the Mets still are not in love with him. He is too easy a target for all the frustrations of what Kranepool himself calls "a seven-year losing streak."

Kranepool's name, floating over the P.A. system in the middle of the lineup, the sixth spot in the order, inspires a chorus of boos.

2:03 p.m.

Jerry Koosman walks to the dugout from the bullpen. He has finished warming up. He is sweating, but his blue Met

27

jacket is buttoned all the way up to the neck. "One thing a shoulder injury does for you," he says. "It teaches you to protect your arm at all times."

2:05 p.m.

Above the field, behind home plate, Bob Murphy, one of the Mets' radio and television announcers, is telling everyone who stayed home from work to watch the telecast that he did the right thing: This is a very important baseball game. Murphy's voice is picked up in New York, New Jersey, Connecticut and, for the first time, in Maine. The Met network has been extended to Maine temporarily so that the president of the ball club, Joan Whitney Payson, vacationing at the Elizabeth Arden health farm, can watch the very important game. All three Cub games, in fact, will be beamed to Elizabeth Arden's at Mrs. Payson's expense. She can afford it.

Mrs. Payson, the wife of financier Charles Payson and sister of John Hay Whitney, formerly the United States Ambassador to the Court of St. James, does not like to miss her Mets. At the start of their first season in 1962, when she traveled to Greece with her daughter and son-in-law, she had the scores cabled to her. After a while, the news grew so depressing that she fired back a cable: PLEASE TELL US ONLY WHEN METS WIN.

"That was the last word I heard from America," she later reported.

2:07 p.m.

Don Kessinger, the first Cub batter, dumps a perfect bunt toward second base. It bounds past Jerry Koosman. Wayne Garrett, a rookie second baseman, sweeps the ball up barehanded perfectly and, in the same motion, throws to first. Kessinger beats the throw.

Glenn Beckert, an excellent bunter, sacrifices Kessinger to second and, quickly, the Cubs have a runner in scoring position. Kessinger, standing on second base, turns to one of the Met infielders. "Our three and four hitters haven't done anything for us in weeks," he says.

The three and four hitters, Billy Williams and Ron Santo, do nothing now. Jerry Koosman strikes out the lean, graceful Williams with a good fast ball at the knees, then, working carefully to Santo, walks him.

Ernie Banks steps up, first in the National League in good humor and third in runs batted in. The crowd, which has swelled to 55,096, the brink of capacity, grows quiet. But seated behind home plate, a fan in his late twenties, dressed in a white polka-dot shirt and sandals, screams, "Strike him out, strike him out."

Koosman gets ahead of Banks, one ball, two strikes. The fan is standing now, pleading, "Strike him out, Jerry, strike him out."

Koosman fires a fast ball on the outside corner, and Banks swings.

The man in the polka-dot shirt jumps up and down, announcing the result, "See, he did it! He did it!"

Koosman has struck out Banks.

2:16 p.m.

Ferguson Jenkins, his fast ball blazing, his curve breaking sharply, dismisses the first three Met batters on ten pitches. He strikes out two, gets the other man on a harmless infield grounder.

2:25 p.m.

When Jerry Koosman gets a full count, three balls, two strikes, on Randy Hundley, the Cubs' leadoff batter in the second inning, umpire Shag Crawford walks out to the mound to examine Koosman's glove and hands, searching for illegal traces of pine tar. Koosman is clean. "I don't know why he checked me so early in the game," Koosman says later. "That's when I was having so much trouble getting anything on the ball. He should have checked me in the middle innings, when I was pitching better."

Koosman walks Hundley, and, in the stands, Richie Parsons, a Met fanatic from Long Island, drains a beer and begins a private monologue. "Ah, damn, he gave up a walk to Hundley. C'mon, Koos, Hickman's up, let's get a double play . . ."

Hickman slams a hard ground ball toward third. "There's the double-play ball," says Parsons, starting a fresh beer.

The ground ball bounces off the chest of Bobby Pfeil, the forty-first man in eight years to play third base for the Mets. Both runners are safe, and Hickman is credited with a single.

"Aw, c'mon, Pfeil, don't mess up chances like that. I'd like a triple play, but it's not damn likely . . ."

29

Two thirteen-year-old Met fans from Brooklyn unfurl a banner and begin a march through the grandstand. The banner reads: TODAY THE METS GRADUATE; TOMORROW THEY SHALL REIGN.

Koosman's first pitch to Don Young is called a ball. "The umps know they're on TV today," says Parsons, finishing his second beer of the inning. "Boy, are they bad!"

Koosman strikes out Young on the next three pitches.

"Got him . . . got him . . . got him. All right. C'mon, sit down in front. C'mon, Koos, get a double play. Jenkins can't hit. Bear down, Koos! C'mon, you can do it. Strike one! All right! C'mon, Jerry, pitch to him. There's a grounder to short. Let's get two . . ."

But Ferguson Jenkins' ground ball to deep shortstop goes for another infield hit. The bases are loaded with one out.

"Please bear down, Jerry, please. Let's get out of the inning." Parsons gulps deep into his third beer of the inning, and Koosman strikes out Kessinger.

"One more, baby, one more, Koos, don't let me down."

Beckert flies deep to right, and Art Shamsky, the best Jewish outfielder in New York since the Dodgers' Cal Abrams—and the first, and the slowest—ambles back to the screen in front of the Met bullpen, reaches up and makes the catch. The inning is over.

In section twelve, behind third base, Joe Delberti, a Met fan since their first season, lofts his banner: UNBELIEVABLE.

"Yahoo!" shouts Richie Parsons, polishing off the third beer. "Yahoo! That's the way to go, Jerry. Yahoo!"

3:12 p.m.

It is the last of the fifth inning, a scoreless game, and Ferguson Jenkins has not yet surrendered a single hit. Jenkins strikes out Wayne Garrett, and Ed Kranepool moves to the plate, preceded, as always, by boos. With one strike, Ferguson throws a slider, and Kranepool lofts the ball high to right field. Jim Hickman, the ex-Met, moves back, looks up, moves back a little farther, looks up again and watches the ball sail over the wall. The crowd roars, the Mets lead, 1–0, and Kranepool trots around the bases as easily as if this were the sort of thing he did every day.

3:13 p.m.

As the last of the first-year Mets circles the bases, the first of the original Mets, Hobie Landrith, a catcher who was plucked from the San Francisco Giants at the start of the expansion draft, is perched on the roof of his home outside San Francisco. Landrith, who endured only one season as a Met, is out of baseball now, an automobile dealer. He is painting his roof white and charcoal gray. He reaches for a brush and, accidentally, drops a can of paint. Eluding Landrith's grasp, the can splashes to the ground. "That's one of the reasons the Mets let me go," he says later.

3:17 p.m.

The Mets' 1–0 lead is less than half an inning old, and Ernie Banks picks out a fast ball and drives it over the left-field wall, tying the score. At the end of the inning, as he trots out toward his position at first base, Banks passes Cleon Jones, the Met outfielder. "Boy," says Banks, smiling, "can we hit!"

3:29 p.m.

Jerry Koosman, who has thrown a lot of pitches, is having trouble with his control. He walks Ferguson Jenkins, the opposing pitcher, to start the seventh inning. Don Kessinger sacrifices Jenkins to second, and Glenn Beckert singles to left, scoring Jenkins. The Cubs lead, 2–1.

3:36 p.m.

As Ferguson Jenkins, pitching smoothly, crisply, efficiently, disposes of the heart of the Met batting order, two young brunettes parade through the lower stands with a banner asking a simple, pointed question: WHAT EVER HAPPENED TO MARV THRONEBERRY?

3:37 p.m.

As the banner waves in Shea Stadium, stirring strong memories, if not quite golden ones, Marv E. Throneberry, whose initials and charmingly graceless ineptitude both spelled MET in 1962, is at work in Memphis, Tennessee. Still only thirty-five years old, out of baseball since 1963, Throneberry is calling upon potential new customers for Carl Carson Car and Truck Rentals, not even aware that the Mets are playing an afternoon game against the Cubs. "I just don't get interested in baseball any more," says Throneberry, a sales and public relations specialist, "not till World Series time, anyway." Some of the crueler critics used to say Marv felt the same way when he played for the Mets.

To each new customer he sees, Throneberry hands his business card. Inside the card are the three main telephone numbers of Carl Carson Car and Truck Rentals. The outside of the card has a hole cut in the middle, and through the hole stares a head-and-shoulders portrait of Marv Throneberry in his old Met uniform. The face of the card reads, modestly: EIGHT MILLION NEW YORKERS CALLED HIM MARVELOUS MARV.

3:45 p.m.

With two men out in the top of the eighth, Jim Hickman comes to bat against Jerry Koosman, the old breed Met against the new. Hickman is greeted, familiarly, with boos. He played for the Mets under a strange curse; someone once suggested he had "potential." If he did, he kept it well hidden.

Hickman added nothing to the comedy at Shea Stadium— he didn't drop fly balls; he simply didn't get to them—and little to the drama. Under pressure, in the mini-crises of the past, Hickman always seemed to harm the Mets.

He does it again now in a major crisis. He hits Koosman's first pitch deep into the Chicago bullpen in left field. Hickman trots around the bases, and the Cubs lead, 3–1.

3:52 p.m.

With two out and no one on base in the bottom of the eighth, shortstop Al Weis comes to the plate. If Weis can get a hit —something no Met has managed since Ed Kranepool's home run—manager Gil Hodges will send up a pinch-hitter for the next batter, Jerry Koosman. Koosman, moving up to the on-deck circle, silently hopes that Ferguson Jenkins will retire Weis. Koosman wants to pitch the ninth inning. "I felt bad and I wanted to make up for some of the pitches I'd thrown," Koosman says later.

Weis grounds out to shortstop, pleasing Koosman, disappointing Barbara Weis, a petite brunette who is seated in the lower stands. "You just wait," Barbara Weis tells her in-laws,

Al's parents, who are sitting with her. "The Mets will do it . . . somehow."

At the same moment, Yogi Berra, coaching at first base, calls to Ernie Banks, trotting off the field, "We're gonna get three in the ninth and beat you." Banks does not even turn his head.

3:58 p.m.

Jerry Koosman, still pitching retires the Cubs in order in the ninth inning, and the Mets move in for their final chance. The odds against them seem infinite: Ferguson Jenkins is pitching magnificently, and of the batters coming up for the Mets— a pinch-hitter, Tommie Agee and Bobby Pfeil—only Agee is a proven threat. Yet few fans leave the park; in recent weeks, the Mets have been rallying dramatically. In seasons past, half the crowd would be fleeing to the parking lot, with logic and history on their side.

3:59 p.m.

Walt Michaels, the defensive backfield coach of the New York Jets—the one championship team in New York—sits in his dormitory room at Hofstra College, the Long Island training camp for the football team. Michaels is watching the Mets on television, calmly, all by himself.

4:00 p.m.

Frank Graddock is settled comfortably before the TV set at his home in the Ridgewood section of Queens, not far from Shea Stadium. He is watching the Mets, and, according to later police reports, he has been drinking during the telecast. His wife, Margaret, walks over to the set and switches the channel away from the Met game. It is time for one of her favorite daytime serials, "Dark Shadows," and today she will find out whether Quentin, who carries the curse of the werewolf, will be able to keep the mummy's hand he has pursued through the last few episodes. Frank Graddock doesn't care about Quentin, his curse or the mummy's hand. He wants to see the ninth inning of the ball game, he and his wife begin to argue over the Mets and the monsters.

4:01 p.m.

To start the last of the ninth inning, Gil Hodges sends up a pinch-hitter for Jerry Koosman—Ken Boswell, the regular second baseman who has been sitting out the game with a bruised hand. Boswell, a pull-hitter, is hitting .245, normal by Met standards. Yet Boswell has some power to right-center field, so the Cub outfield plays him deep. Ferguson Jenkins works the count on Boswell to two balls, two strikes. The Mets, newly conditioned to expect the impossible, crowd the front steps of their dugout.

Boswell hits Jenkins' next pitch high into short right-center field. Don Young, the Cub center fielder who plays mainly on the strength of his fielding, hesitates for a moment, waiting for the ball to come out of the haze and background of white shirts in the crowd. He hesitates too long. As he charges in and Don Kessinger and Glenn Beckert pedal back, the ball falls to the ground. Second base is left uncovered, and Boswell alertly stretches his pop fly into a double. The Cubs have committed a combination mental-and-physical error straight out of Met tradition.

4:04 p.m.

On "Dark Shadows," Quentin is faced with an agonizing decision: Should he keep the mummy's paw or return it in exchange for advice from Angelique, a witch, on how to shake the werewolf's curse? Margaret Graddock wants to find out, but her husband insists upon watching a baseball game. She switches the channel; he switches back to Shea Stadium.

4:05 p.m.

With Ken Boswell at second base and the huge crowd chanting for a rally, Tommie Agee, the strong, powerful Met outfielder, slashes a ball past third base, just foul. Ferguson Jenkins misses the plate with his next two pitches, and catcher Randy Hundley goes to the mound to settle him down. In the Cub dugout, Leo Durocher, outwardly unworried, sits with his legs crossed. Agee hits Jenkins' next pitch straight up, and Ernie Banks drifts over by the Met dugout and makes the catch for the first out. Cleon Jones watches from the dugout steps. His mind drifts back to a game earlier in the season, when the Mets came from behind and beat the Atlanta Braves.

4:07 p.m.

Gil Hodges pulls out Bobby Pfeil and sends up Donn Clendenon to pinch-hit. A restaurateur in Atlanta in the off-season,

Clendenon has, he confesses, "a propensity for striking out." He holds the National League record with 163 strikeouts in a single season. But he also has a propensity for hitting a base-ball great distances.

Clendenon moves his hands up on the bat. While a home run would tie the game, Clendenon is hoping mainly to keep the mild rally alive, trying to get the bat on the ball, looking for a single or a double. He drives Ferguson Jenkins' first pitch foul down the right-field line. The next pitch, a curve ball, misses the inside corner.

Jenkins takes a deep breath and throws. Clendenon swings and lines the ball deep toward the left-field wall. The drive sinks, falling short of a home run, and Don Young, the Chicago center fielder, racing full speed, reaches out and snares the ball before it can hit the wall. But Young, the ball resting tentatively in the webbing of his glove, cannot brake. He slams into the fence. The ball pops loose.

Boswell, forced to wait at second to see if the ball will be caught, moves only to third. Clendenon reaches second. The tying runs are in scoring position, and the fans at Shea Stadium are screaming.

4:08 p.m.

Margaret Graddock is screaming, too. She wants to see "Dark Shadows." On the show, Angelique, the witch, is explaining how she was once bitten by a vampire.

Frank Graddock screams back at his wife and starts hitting her, too, the police say later. Reportedly, Frank Graddock punches his wife in the head and body. Angelique, the witch, is about to strangle a man to death. Cleon Jones is about to come to bat.

4:09 p.m.

Cleon Jones moves from the on-deck circle to the plate. He has been hitless all day, still looking for his 100th base hit of the season; he started the day leading the National League in batting, but his average has slipped a few points. "You gotta get a hit now," Jones tells himself. "If you don't, you'll kick yourself all the way home in the car. It's time to do your thing."

Donn Clendenon leads off second base. "Don't get picked off," he tells himself. "If I ever get picked off in front of all these people, I'll kill myself."

Jones watches the first pitch. It is low. Then Ferguson

35

Jenkins throws a curve, which failing to break, hangs over the plate. Jones cracks the ball on a line over third base and into the left-field corner. Before Billy Williams, in left field, can chase the ball down, Ken Boswell and Clendenon have scored, tying the game, and Jones is standing on second base.

The Met players, pouring out of their dugout, devour the two runners, pounding their backs, shaking their fists defiantly at the Cub dugout.

Leo Durocher emerges, walks to the mound, and talks to Jenkins. He leaves his ace in the game.

4:10 p.m.

Walt Michaels' room at Hofstra College is now filled with Jet football players, yelling and shouting, most of them pulling for the Mets. They are almost as excited as they would be if Joe Namath, temporarily in retirement, walked into the training camp.

4:11 p.m.

Leo Durocher, after consulting with Ferguson Jenkins, orders the Mets' clean-up hitter, Art Shamsky, deliberately walked, setting up a possible double-play situation. But the next batter, Wayne Garrett, grounds softly to second base, and Glenn Beckert has to make the play at first, allowing the runners to move up to second and third.

The next batter is Ed Kranepool, greeted by cheers, partly redeemed by his home run.

"C'mon, Everitt," shouts Jack Wakefield, a professional comedian who is sitting behind home plate, a dedicated fan who often treats Met pitchers to dinner after winning performances. "C'mon, Everitt."

Wakefield turns to the people around him. "He hates the name Everitt," says Wakefield. "I call him that to get him mad enough to get a hit."

Kranepool may have regained stature in the eyes of Met fans by his home run, but he has not convinced the Cubs. Rather than walk him and face J. C. Martin, the Met catcher, Durocher and Jenkins decide to pitch to Kranepool.

4:13 p.m.

Frank Graddock is watching the Mets on his television set. His wife, Margaret, is lying in bed, nursing the injuries she

36

allegedly suffered trying to get to see "Dark Shadows." Her husband concentrates upon the game, unaware that his wife is fatally hurt, unaware that he will be charged the following day, with first-degree murder.

4:14 p.m.

Ed Kranepool lugs a 36-ounce bat to the plate, several ounces heavier than the one he customarily uses. A heavier bat has helped the hitting of both Cleon Jones and Donn Clendenon. "You can't argue with success," Kranepool says later.

Ferguson Jenkins' first pitch is high. Kranepool watches the next one for a strike and misses the third.

The crowd is on its feet. Kranepool digs in. He notices that shortstop Don Kessinger is playing him towards second base, leaving lots of room through the left side to the infield. Kranepool is expecting an outside pitch—but not the one Jenkins throws him. It is outside and low, and Kranepool fooled, practically throws his bat at the ball. The bat connects. The ball bloops out toward left field, over the head of Kessinger.

Cleon Jones dances down the line, jumping every few feet, as he scores the winning run. Jerry Koosman, suddenly the winning pitcher, is the first to greet Jones, hugging him, lifting him off the ground. Mets hug each other all over the field. In the record books, it will read simply as a 4–3 victory over the Chicago Cubs on a July afternoon. But, for the Mets, it is, for an instant, the seventh game of an imaginary world series.

Upstairs, in the television booth, announcer Lindsey Nelson is screaming. "It's absolute bedlam. You could not believe it. It's absolute bedlam."

In the stands, Barbara Weis points her finger at her in-laws. "See," she says. "I told you they'd do it . . . somehow."

Near Barbara Weis, in a beige-and-brown sleeveless dress, Lavonne Koosman sits, tears streaming down her face and smearing her make-up.

4:20 p.m.

Joseph Ignac of Elizabeth, New Jersey, heads out of Shea Stadium, starting his two-hour trip home. Never once, in his eight seasons of cheering for the Mets, has he felt so good. For the first time, he doesn't miss Willie Mays quite so much.

4:22 p.m.

The Met clubhouse is alive with cries of "Attaboy, attaboy," uncommon in a professional baseball locker room. The clubhouse policemen are working furiously to cope with the flood of reporters trying to fight their way to the happy players.

"Passes, passes," one policeman calls. "Any ringers here? Any ringers?"

Cleon Jones, Donn Clendenon and Ed Kranepool are delayed, busy chatting on the Mets' post-game television show, "Kiner's Corner," with the host, Ralph Kiner, a home-run hitter turned broadcaster. The press focuses on Jerry Koosman, who is sitting, dazed, in front of his locker, mumbling, "Unbelievable, unbelievable."

Koosman gulps down a can of Rheingold, brewed by the Mets' sponsors, and drags on a cigarette. "They were marvelous," he says, indicating his teammates. "I was wild all day. I felt sure of myself, but I didn't have good control. I was battling myself."

The home-run pitches to Ernie Banks and Jim Hickman, Koosman says, were both fast balls—slow fast balls. "My best fast ball," he says, "would have gotten there two feet sooner."

"Do you think the club's going all the way now?" says one reporter.

"Pardon?"

The reporter repeats the question.

Koosman smiles, and, playing the game, replies, "I don't see why we just can't keep on winning and winning."

4:23 p.m.

In the Chicago clubhouse, Don Young the outfielder, is dressing as fast as he possibly can. "If I value my life," he tells himself, "I'll get the hell out of here."

Several of the Cub players, like friends paying a condolence call, drift over to Young's locker and tell him to forget about the two mistakes he made, not to worry about them. A few suggest that he get himself a drink quickly.

Back in the manager's room, Leo Durocher is opening up to reporters. "That kid in center field," he says to the Chicago writers. "Two little fly balls. He just stands there watching one, and he gives up on the other." Durocher flavors his remarks with his choicest obscenities, and Durocher is a master of the idiom.

38

"If a man can't catch a fly ball," Durocher says, "you don't deserve to win."

The manager glances toward Ferguson Jenkins, who is slumped in front of his locker. "Look at him," Durocher says. "He threw his heart out. You won't see a better-pitched game. And that kid in center field gives it away on him. It's a disgrace."

4:29 p.m.

Ron Santo, the Cub third baseman, is no more charitable than his manager. "He was just thinking about himself, not the team," says Santo, angrily, referring to Don Young. "He had a bad day at the bat, so he's got his head down. He's worrying about his batting average and not the team. All right, he can keep his head down, and he can keep right on going, out of sight for all I care. We don't need that kind of thing."

Santo slams his spikes against the floor. "I don't know who Leo has in mind to play center field," he says, "but I hope I can sell him on Hickman. Any ball Jim reaches, you can bet your money he'll hold onto."

4:35 p.m.

Cleon Jones has returned from the post-game show and now, in response to questions, he is reliving the ninth inning. "The Cubs went out there patting their pockets when they took the field in the ninth," says Jones. "They were already started to count that twenty-five grand." He smiles, thinking himself of the potential share for each championship player in the upcoming intra-league championship series and the World Series.

"Banks, he talks to you all the time," Jones says. "He kept saying to me over and over, 'That Jenkins, he can really pitch.' I didn't give up. Nobody gave up. This is a young club and it believes it can win. We've got the momentum now."

Jones looks toward Tom Seaver, who is scheduled to pitch for the Mets tomorrow. "We beat their big man," says Jones. "Now we've got our big man. We're in command now. We can relax."

"Hey, don't save the fireworks until the ninth inning for me," says Seaver. "I'll take a 9–0 lead in the first inning any time. I'll finesse it the rest of the way."

4:37 p.m.

Ron Santo is still fuming in the Chicago locker room. "It's ridiculous," he says. "There's no way the Mets can beat us. Just no way. It's a shame losing to an infield like that. Why, I wouldn't let that infield play in Tacoma."

4:42 p.m.

The Met locker room is starting to thin out. Ed Charles, a veteran third baseman who saw no action, is chatting with a couple of reporters. "If we can only just hang close to the Cubs until September . . . ," he says.

4:43 p.m.

Ferguson Jenkins has no abuse for Don Young. "With all those people here on a bright day," the pitcher says, "the center fielder is in a constant battle with the sun. I thought Young recovered quickly. After all, he had to find it before he could chase it." Young doesn't hear the words in his defense. He has fled from the clubhouse.

4:50 p.m.

Harold Weissman, the publicity director of the Mets, a very serious reformed newspaperman, is standing with Jerry Koosman. "What an ending, what an ending," says Weissman, still dazed.

Then, thinking about the heart attack Gil Hodges suffered late in the 1968 season, Weissman says, "What do you think Gil's doctor said about that finish?"

"Maybe we'd better pay to have the doctor here," says Koosman, kidding.

"Yeah," says Weissman, his face totally serious. "Yeah."

5:10 p.m.

At Camp Drum in Watertown, New York, Sergeant Derrel McKinley Harrelson is getting ready to umpire a softball game between two teams of Army reservists. When he isn't putting in his two weeks of summer training, Sergeant Harrelson is Bud Harrelson, the regular shortstop for the New York Mets.

Sergeant Harrelson is umpiring because he fears that, if he played softball, he might lose his batting groove. It is not one of the greatest grooves of baseball—Harrelson, an accomplished fielder, is a confirmed .220 to .240 hitter—but it is the only one he has.

"Your club scored three runs in the ninth and won," somebody says.

Harrelson laughs. He is used to being kidded in his outfit. The previous week, when the Mets won six out of nine games from St. Louis and Pittsburgh without him, his army buddies teased him about his indispensability. Harrelson is a pleasant young man, and he takes jokes well.

"Sure, we got three in the ninth," he says. He had heard earlier that the Mets were losing, 3–1, going into the ninth.

"Hey, sarge," someone else yells from the barracks. "You won, 4–3."

Suddenly, Harrelson realizes he is not being kidded. He breaks into a big grin and, in fatigues, begins umpiring a meaningless softball game.

6:00 p.m.

Ed Kranepool walks into the bar at Tavern on the Green, a restaurant in Central Park. He is accompanied by Howard Cosell, the sportscaster, who is going to interview him on ABC-TV's 6:30 news.

As the two men enter, the bartenders begin to applaud.

Cosell nods gently, presuming, as he always does, that the cheers are for him and his syntax.

"Champagne, Mr. Kranepool?" says one of the bartenders.

"No," says Kranepool. "Just straight Beefeaters on the rocks, with just a touch of vermouth."

Kranepool will save the champagne for the World Series.

6:20 p.m.

Donn Clendenon notices a crowd around the entrance to his apartment on West 58th Street. He recognizes no one, but as he approaches, the people cluster around him, slapping him on the back, cheering him, congratulating him. "These people," he says to himself, "they're talking pennant fever too early for me."

6:40 p.m.

Eddie Yost, the third-base coach who waved Cleon Jones home with the winning run, returns to his house. He looks

41

quickly around the house. To his relief, he sees that the huge black dog that haunted his morning has been returned to its owner.

"I can't see having a pet," says Yost. "Not with us going to Florida in the spring for seven weeks."

7:30 p.m.

At the Dragonseed Restaurant in Queens, Albert "Rube" Walker, the round, cheerful pitching coach of the Mets, is eating dinner with Verlon "Rube" Walker, the round, cheerful third-base coach of the Cubs. The two brothers do not talk much about the game or about the pennant race. Later, when Albert "Rube" is asked if he and Verlon "Rube" might split any potential World Series share, the Mets' Walker says, "Hell, no. I'm not going halves. I need the money more than he does."

7:38 p.m.

The other New York team loses the opening game of a twi-night doubleheader and falls eighteen and a half games out of first place.

7:45 p.m.

Phil Rizzuto, who broadcasts the games of the other team, is interviewing Mrs. Babe Ruth between the halves of the doubleheader. It is "Babe Ruth Day" in Baltimore, and Mrs. Ruth is talking about her husband's birthplace, which has been turned into a museum.

Rizzuto, once the Yankee shortstop, still clings to the Yankees, but Mrs. Ruth is more up-to-date. She is a Met fan. "I think they're adorable," she told a reporter only yesterday. "I love every one of them. I cry when they lose and I laugh when they win."

7:50 p.m.

In a room at the Waldorf-Astoria Hotel in Manhattan, Rich Nye, a young left-handed pitcher, is trying to cheer up his Cub roommate, Don Young. But, although he has had a couple of drinks, Young is still depressed. He has been a professional baseball player since he was seventeen, in 1963, but he has never hit .300, not even in the Pioneer League or the California League or the Texas League. His batting average with the

CUBS vs. METS at SHEA STADIUM DATE JULY 8, 1969

PLAYER		1	2	3	4	5	6	7	8	9	10	11	12	AB	BB	R	H	RBI	SO	PO	A	E
KESSINGER	6													4	0	1	0	0	0	1	2	1	0
BECKERT	4													4	0	2	0	1	0	0	1	5	1	0
WILLIAMS	7													4	0	1	0	0	0	1	3	0	0
SANTO	5													3	0	0	1	0	0	0	0	3	0
BANKS	3													4	1	1	0	1	0	1	0	7	0
HUNDLEY	2													2	0	0	2	0	0	0	6	0	0
HICKMAN	9													4	1	2	0	0	0	3	0	0	0
YOUNG	8													4	0	0	0	2	0	1	0	0
JENKINS	1													3	1	1	0	0	1	0	0	1	1
TOTALS														32	3	9	3	0	6	2	21	8	1

2 base hits

3 base hits

Home runs: BANKS, HICKMAN

Double plays

Bases on balls, off: JENKINS-1

Struck out by: JENKINS-8

Innings pitch by: JENKIN-8⅓

Earned runs by: JENKINS-4

Opponents' hits at: JENKINS-5

Wild pitches: 0

Balk: 0

Passed balls: 0

Winning pitcher: KOOSMAN (9-3)

Losing pitcher: JENKINS (11-6)

Umpires

Score

Time of game 2:09

43

METS vs. CUBS at SHEA STADIUM DATE July 8, 1969

PLAYER	1	2	3	4	5	6	7	8	9	10	11	12	AB	R	H				PA	A	E	
AGEE	8												4	0	0	0	0	0	3	0	0	1 base hit BOSWELL, CLENDENON, JONES
CLENDENON - ph	5												1	1	1	0	0	0	0	0	0	2 base hits
PFEIL	7												3	0	0	0	0	0	1	2	0	Home run KRANEPOOL
JONES	7												4	1	1	0	2	0	2	0	0	Double play PFEIL-GARRETT-KRANEPOOL
SHAMSKY	9												3	0	0	0	1	0	0	0	0	Bases on balls off KOOSMAN - 4
GARRETT	4												4	0	0	0	0	0	0	3	0	Struck out by KOOSMAN - 6
KRANEPOOL	3												4	1	2	0	2	0	1	0	0	Innings pitch by KOOSMAN - 9
MARTIN	2												3	0	0	0	0	1	8	0	0	Earned runs off KOOSMAN - 3
WEISS	6												3	0	0	0	0	0	1	2	0	Opponents hits off KOOSMAN - 8
BOSWELL - ph													2	0	1	0	0	0	0	0	0	Wild pitch 0
KOOSMAN	1																					Passed balls 0
																						Winning pitcher KOOSMAN (6-5)
																						Losing pitcher BURNS (11-4)
																						Umpires PELEKOUDAS, HARVEY, DEZELAN, CRAWFORD
TOTALS													32	4	5	1	4	0	26	9	0	Scorer
																						Time of game 2:09

Cubs now has sunk to .228, and his glove has betrayed him. His phone rings. Rick Talley, a Chicago columnist, is calling. Talley wants to know if Young lost Ken Boswell's pop fly in the white shirts of the crowd.

"I don't know," says Young. "I don't know."

Did his performance at the plate—two strikeouts and two pop flies—affect his defensive play?

"No," says Young. "I just lost the game for us. That's all."

Talley finishes the interview and taps out his column: "Young has a history of 'getting down' on himself. He is not a confident ballplayer. He has been happy with the Cubs, but never quite believed it and always seemed to be wondering when it was going to end. It may have ended yesterday."

10:22 p.m.

The other New York team loses the second game of a twi-night doubleheader and falls nineteen and a half games out of first place.

11:00 p.m.

The first edition of the *New York Times* goes on sale on the streets of the city. The story of the Mets' rally is on the front page of the newspaper. The Mets have been on the front page before, but only once for winning a ball game, way back in 1962, when, after nine consecutive defeats, they scored the first victory of their existence.

Two

The Day Tom Seaver Was Almost Perfect

WEDNESDAY
JULY 9, 1969

NATIONAL LEAGUE STANDINGS
Eastern Division

	W	L	PCT.	G.B.
Chicago	52	32	.619	—
New York	46	34	.575	4
St. Louis	41	44	.482	11½
Pittsburgh	39	43	.476	12
Philadelphia	36	44	.450	14
Montreal	26	56	.317	25

By the middle of the 1965 National League season, the New York Mets had learned to loathe the Houston Astros. In theory, the Mets and the Astros, like all men, had been created equal, each team drawn in 1962 from the most tired cast-offs and the least promising prospects the other National League clubs were willing to surrender. In theory, the Mets and the Astros should have been giving each other a good fight to determine the worst team in baseball history. But, in practice, the Mets had already clinched the title. In the first three years of their existence, Houston had finished ahead of New York every season, and the Astros had won two out of every three games between the clubs.

On July 9, 1965, the Mets and Astros met in Shea Stadium, and, for the seventh straight time that season, Houston won. The Astros won, 6–2, behind the pitching of a teenager, a rookie named Larry Dierker; they wrapped up the game with five runs in the second inning, when the Mets' second baseman dropped a pop fly and the Mets' shortstop made a wild throw. The Mets' second baseman was Chuck Hiller, so accomplished a fielder he was nicknamed "Dr. No," after the ironhanded James Bond villain; the shortstop was Roy McMillan, a remarkable fielder in his twenties, who joined the Mets in his thirties.

The other Met star of the day was Gordon Richardson, a left-handed pitcher, whose first pitch, since being recalled from Buffalo in the International League, was hit for a triple.

In 1968—two years after Richardson and McMillan ended their Met careers, one year after Hiller ended his Met career—the New York Mets, for the first time in their history, finished ahead of the Houston Astros.

8:30 a.m.

Ed Kranepool, who for years was allowed to sleep as late as he wished—some people said he didn't wake up till the end of the ninth inning—is awakened by a phone call from George Matson, a New York Daily News photographer. Matson wants to take pictures of Kranepool, his wife, Carole, and their four-month-old son, Edward Keith Kranepool. "A year ago," says Kranepool, "they couldn't give away pictures of me."

The phone keeps ringing in the Kranepools' Long Island home. "This is what happens when you're winning," he says. "People call you for tickets. People drop by to say hello and offer congratulations. This hasn't happened in seven years.

We've caught everybody by surprise. And, frankly, we weren't that sure of ourselves, either."

10:00 a.m.

Tom Seaver wakes up on schedule, after precisely nine and a half hours of sleep, just the amount of rest he likes the night before he is going to pitch. He had stayed up till 12:30 the previous night chatting with his father, Charles Seaver, once an outstanding amateur golfer, who is visiting from California. The Seavers had watched the Yankees play Baltimore on television, and when Baltimore had scored its tenth run of the second game, Charles Seaver had said, "My God, the Yankees look like the Mets used to."

Charles Seaver's son is the best reason the Mets no longer look the same. Tom Seaver, who will face the Cubs tonight, has won seven games in a row, bringing his 1969 record to 13–3. In his two and a half seasons with the Mets, he has won a total of forty-five games, more than any other pitcher in the club's history, more than the whole team won its first season. He is the Mets' first superstar, and they acquired him only through another team's error.

In 1966, while Seaver was pitching for the University of Southern California, the Atlanta Braves gave him a $50,000 bonus. Atlanta's judgment was fine, but its timing was off. By signing Seaver after the start of his college season and before he graduated, the Braves violated one of the rules of organized baseball. The Commissioner of Baseball nullified the contract and announced that any team willing to match the Braves' bonus price could compete in a drawing for Seaver.

The Mets were interested. "I was the guy who told the Mets about Tom," says Dick Selma, a former Met pitcher who is now with the Cubs. Selma and Seaver grew up together in Fresno, California, and for many years, in Little League and high-school competition, Selma was the star and Seaver just another pitcher. But Seaver matured, as an athlete, in college. "I told Al Lyons (a Met scout) that this kid could pitch in the biggies when Tom was at USC," says Selma. "I knew he was ready 'cause I knew what he had *inside*. He's a good pitcher now, but he's really no better than when he came up. That's how good he was to start with."

In the drawing, the Mets won the rights to Seaver, the first brilliant move they had ever made, on the field or off. Seaver spent one season in the minor leagues, winning twelve games and losing twelve at Jacksonville in the International League, then reported to the major-league camp in 1967. It didn't take him long to prove himself. He was the best pitcher ever to wear a Met uniform as soon as he put on a Met uniform. He won sixteen games on a tenth-place team and was named the National League's rookie of the year; in 1968, he won sixteen games again.

Seaver is educated, amiable, articulate, which separates him from the majority, and he is also a very practical young man. He does not believe at all in superstition. He will wear blue socks for one victory and brown ones for the next, loafers one victory and dress shoes the next; he is not afraid to change anything except his pitching style. "What could wearing the same shorts to the mound," he says, "have to do with pitching?"

Instead of superstition, Seaver relies on sound physical preparation (twelve hours of sleep two nights before the game, then nine and a half the night before the game), sound mental preparation (he thinks about the opposing hitters "enough but not too much") and, most of all, a complete repertoire of pitches—fast ball, curve, slider, change-up, all thrown with magnificent control. Most games, one or two of his deliveries is exceptional, and he will concentrate on those pitches. "Two or three times a year," he says, "I can throw the ball just where I want, as hard as I want, with just the right motion. Two or three times a year, you put it all together."

12:10 p.m.

The *Daily News* photographer has arrived at Ed Kranepool's home and is taking pictures of Tuesday's hero, his wife and son. At four months of age, Edward Keith Kranepool already weighs seventeen pounds. "I hope he's a righthander," says his left-handed father. "Then I'll make him a switch-hitter. His father's been platooned for seven years. I want him to play every day."

1:00 p.m.

Tommie Agee is in the middle of Central Park, a set of headphones and a microphone strapped to his head. He and three of his Met teammates—Rod Gaspar, Al Weis and Jerry Koosman—are conducting a baseball clinic. Rows and rows of teenaged boys are sitting on benches, listening to Agee's tips

on hitting, trying to learn something. A year ago, they would have been trying not to laugh.

In 1968, Tommie Agee led the Mets only in disappointment, a very painful statistic, because in order to get Agee from the Chicago White Sox before the season, the Mets gave up the men who led them in 1967 in nine different batting categories and five different pitching categories—Tommy Davis and Jack Fisher. Davis led in the nine batting categories, an impressive list including hits, runs, doubles, home runs, runs batted in and average. Fisher led in the five pitching categories, a less impressive list including hits allowed, runs allowed, home runs allowed and defeats.

The Mets were willing to surrender Davis and Fisher (and a third man no one remembers) for Agee and Al Weis largely because of Agee's potential. In 1966, he was the American League's rookie of the year, batting .273 with twenty-two home runs. The White Sox found him expendable when his average dropped thirty-nine points in 1967.

Still, to the Mets, he looked like the center fielder they had been searching for ever since Richie Ashburn retired in 1963. (Ashburn, who was thirty-five when he joined the Mets, several steps slower than in his prime years with the Philadelphia Phillies, still led the original Met club with a .306 batting average.)

Everything went wrong for Agee when he joined the Mets. His first time up in spring training, against the St. Louis Cardinals, he was struck on the head by a pitch from Bob Gibson, who throws hard. During the regular season, Agee did manage to tie one Met record; he went thirty-four times at bat in a row without a hit, tying the mark set by an original Met, Don Zimmer, who had been hit in the head by pitched balls a few times during his major-league career. Zimmer, by the time he joined the Mets, at least had the excuse of poor vision.

The more Agee tried, the worse he played. He struck out more often than he hit safely. He took to arriving at the ball park as late as possible and leaving right after the game. He was lonely and miserable. His batting average sank to .217. "I wanted to explode when the season ended," he recalls. "The Mets sent me to Florida to work on my hitting, but after one week I told them I just had to get away. So I took two dozen baseballs, went home to Mobile and spent the winter thinking."

In Alabama, Agee saw a lot of Cleon Jones, his fellow Met and his former high-school teammate in football, basketball and baseball. (Agee went to Grambling College on a football scholarship.) "Every morning Cleon and I would go out in a little boat and fish and talk about hitting," Agee says. "Then, in the afternoon, Tommy Aaron of the Atlanta Braves would come over and we'd go out to a playground and hit those two dozen balls around. And this spring in Florida, every time I'd bat, Cleon would tell me what I was doing wrong."

This season Agee hasn't done much wrong. "The Old Mets are dead," he said after his double enabled New York to rally and beat San Diego, 3–2, on June 8. "The New Breed is here, baby. I brought it here with me. It took me a year to get it going, but it's here."

Agee is hitting .279 now and leading the Mets in home runs with twelve. He is fully qualified to show teenagers how to swing a bat.

Of course, not everyone in Central Park is watching Agee. In the distance, couples lie on the grass sunning themselves and other couples lie on the grass not sunning themselves. Even among the crowd on the benches in front of Agee, Gaspar, Weis and Koosman, a middle-aged woman, oblivious to the Mets, is buried deep in the *Daily News*. Two youngsters in Met uniforms jump up in front of her. "Sit down, boys, sit down," she says, automatically. When the boys sit down, she returns to her paper, not looking up until the clinic is over.

But another woman, a gray-haired lady of sixty-seven, is more attentive. "Did you learn anything?" someone asks her as the players leave.

"Sure," says the woman, "I learned how to field a ground ball from Al Weis."

2:30 p.m.

Billy Williams, the Chicago outfielder, ventures into the lobby of the Waldorf-Astoria Hotel. The lobby is dense with the youngsters who always haunt the hotels where baseball clubs stay, youngsters searching for autographs. Williams calls them "lobby rats," and they have no trouble spotting him. Aside from his obvious grace and athletic build, tall black men in pea-green suits are not common at the Waldorf. The lobby rats approach him near the newsstand.

"Go away," Williams says. "I sign at the ballpark." Then he relents and scribbles his name on a couple of notepads. Suddenly, he breaks away from the kids. He has spotted an old friend who played with him in the Sooner State League in 1956.

"Flash . . . woweee . . . Flash!" Williams says.

"How you been, Billy?" says Howard "Flash" Gordon, a Panamanian who, at thirty-eight, now lives in Brooklyn and works in the accounting department of the Mobil Oil Company. Gordon and Williams sit down and reminisce for a while. When Gordon leaves, Williams slouches back on the couch, thinking.

"Flash never got a break," he says, quietly. "He hit over .300 three times and never got a break. That must be tough, to never get a break."

2:35 p.m.

A small pack of reporters from the Chicago newspapers file into a suite on the tenth floor of the Waldorf to attend Ron Santo's press conference. Dressed in a black knit sports shirt and checkered-black-and-white slacks, the slightly balding third baseman sits down on the edge of his bed.

"Don Young and I talked for an hour today," he begins. "I apologized to him then and I want to make a public apology now for what I said yesterday. I was upset. There had been a lot of pressure before the game from newsmen, radio and television. Then we lost the game the way we did and when I saw Donnie walking out of the clubhouse five minutes after the game was over, I just lost my head. I said he'd put his head down between his legs because of his hitting. I was wrong. I said it because it had happened to me when I was on a losing ball club. I fought myself so hard at the plate that when I went to the field I forgot about fielding and I caused the team to lose ball games. I thought the same thing had happened to Donnie, but it really didn't."

Santo pauses. "Donnie has done too much for us," he says. "He's too good a kid and too good a competitor. You've got to be a competitor to get as mad as he got at himself yesterday. He walked out of the clubhouse because he couldn't bear to face his teammates.

"We had a long talk. Very, very emotional. I knew I was wrong. I couldn't sleep last night thinking about it. I tried to convince myself that I was right but I knew I wasn't."

3:00 p.m.

Rube Walker, the New York Rube Walker, is getting ready to leave the Traveler's Motel, a temporary home for many of the Mets. He has been getting phone calls all day from old and new friends, all congratulating him, all requesting the same thing—tickets for tonight's game. Each player is allotted six free tickets a game, and Walker has already given away four of his to Joe Pignatano, who also has discovered he has a lot of friends.

Just before he leaves for Shea Stadium, Walker is handed a message at the desk. The bellboy wants two tickets. "Gee, I hate to disappoint him," says Walker. "He runs us over to the park and takes care of our stuff when we're away."

3:30 p.m.

Tommie Agee, finished with his classes in Central Park, walks into the Deerhead Restaurant, not far from Shea Stadium. Like most athletes, he tries to eat his pre-game meal at least four hours before game time, and, like most people, he prefers to eat a meal without being disturbed. Up till now, he has been able to eat in peace at the Deerhead.

A waitress walks over and asks for Agee's order, and as he looks up, a little boy across the restaurant notices him. "Hey!" the boy calls. "That's Agee!"

Agee winces.

The cook wanders out to the counter opposite Agee's table and stands there. The waitresses decide they need a break and loiter around nearby booths. The boy who spotted Agee moves to a table facing his. No one says a word, but everyone stares.

When Agee looks up, the cook, the waitresses and the boy turn away. Agee squirms. "I guess I won't be able to eat *here* again," he says.

4:00 p.m.

At the Shea Stadium parking lot, a worn Oldsmobile pulls into the spot reserved for the manager, Gil Hodges. The manager steps out, and so does his chauffeur, coach Joe Pignatano. As he heads into the stadium, Hodges glances at Pignatano's car. "I'm not saying it's old," he says. "Let's just say that Piggy is getting a new car soon."

The arrangement between the manager and the coach— taking turns driving to the ball park—is about to face a crisis; Pignatano is moving soon from Brooklyn, Hodges' home, to Staten Island. "I don't want to be one-way about this," the manager says, with a straight face, "but it seems to me that Piggy can continue to pick me up on his day. On my day—I think Piggy is going to have to drive himself."

Hodges permits himself a smile. "But I don't want to be one-way about this," he repeats.

Hodges is a needler, with a sly sense of humor. Earlier in the season, when a reporter asked him if he were going to call the Mets "a team of destiny," he said, "No, but I will if you want me to."

He is, outwardly, a very calm, very controlled man, partly by inclination and, now, partly by necessity. He suffered a heart attack in Atlanta late in the 1968 season, and after a winter of recuperation, he showed up at the Mets' 1969 training camp a serious, cautious figure. He walked slowly and worked himself carefully into the drills and routine of the spring camp.

Hodges paced himself delicately through a Met training camp once before, in 1963, when he was coming off a winter knee operation. He was a player then, reaching the end of a brilliant career that included eleven straight seasons of hitting twenty or more home runs for the Brooklyn and Los Angeles Dodgers, appearances in seven World Series and eight nominations to the National League All-Star team. He was a first baseman, a converted catcher, and, at six-foot-two and 200 pounds, he was immensely powerful. But, by 1963, his knee could not carry him through another year. He went to bat for the Mets only twenty-two times in the regular season before he was offered the job of managing the Washington Senators.

In his first six years as a manager, five with Washington and one with the Mets, Hodges' teams never escaped from the second division. Yet, each year, his teams won more games than they had the previous year. Because of that modest accomplishment, and because of his image—he has been the quiet hero, the humble, gentle giant, ever since his Dodger days—he is as secure as a losing manager can be.

Now, for the first time, he has a team threatening to finish above .500. He is in the middle of a pressure series in a pressure season, and he is bantering easily with friends, smiling most of the time, shaking the after-effects of his heart attack. When the Mets won eleven straight games last month, Hodges,

who respects baseball's superstitions, hit infield practice for twelve straight days, until the club lost.

Today, the Mets are risking a six-game winning streak against the Cubs, and Rube Walker will hit infield practice for the seventh straight day.

4:20 p.m.

Rube Walker sits at a table in the middle of the Met clubhouse signing cards shaped like baseballs. He will be giving them away to the fans who come to see him in the Met autograph room at 7:00 P.M. The Mets take turns playing host as part of the club's fan club nights.

Rube signs eight or nine cards.

"That ought to be enough," needles Ken Boswell, standing nearby with a towel slung over his shoulder.

Walker scowls at Boswell and signs fifty more cards. "I'm not signing another damn one of these," says Walker. He smiles and keeps on signing. Then he remembers that infield drill starts at 7:35.

"I'm going to tell the fans that I've got to leave early so we can keep the streak going," he says. Then, with a grin, he adds, "It's a good excuse not to stay long."

4:35 p.m.

Ken Boswell sits in front of his locker reading a newspaper account of the fight between Frank Graddock and his wife that led to her death. "That's funny," Boswell says. "That's funny . . . in a tragic sort of way."

4:45 p.m.

Tommie Agee is chatting about Joe Namath, the New York Jets' quarterback who has temporarily retired from football. "I met him at Bachelors III one day last winter," says Agee, himself a bachelor. "I go up to him and introduce myself. He's sitting at the bar with a beautiful girl on his right. She's dressed in chinchilla. Joe leans over to me after a while and, you know, he's talking to me like a hippie or something.

" 'You know, Tommie,' he says. 'I've got a problem, I'm in a fix. You see this girl on my right. Well, she's waiting to go home with me. You see that girl over there, that blonde, well, she's waiting for me to take her home. You see that girl at the end of the bar. Well, she's waiting for me to take her home. But that's not all. I just got a phone call from my girl friend and she says she's on the way down here.' "

57

Agee shakes his head. "Well," he says, "Joe says he's got a problem. I mean, I'd like to have a problem like that."

4:47 p.m.

Gus Mauch, the Mets' trainer who previously served the New York Yankees through eleven World Series, walks over to Rube Walker's locker. Walker has finished signing the baseball cards.

"You interested in going up to Grossinger's on the next off day?" Mauch asks him. "You only pay for the tips and drinks. The rooms and meals are free."

Grossinger's is a resort in the Catskills that offers its guests a Kosher cuisine, a daily session of "Simon Says," and an occasional glimpse of a visiting celebrity. The celebrities tend to run to ballplayers and Broadway columnists.

"C'mon, roomie," says Joe Pignatano. "Say you'll go. It's a good tip."

Then Pignatano turns to Mauch. "But everything isn't free," he says. "It costs to play golf. It cost me $28 to play a round."

"Well," Mauch concedes, "everything is free but the tips and drinks and *golf*. Do you want me to put you down?"

"And I had to pay $8 for a cart," says Pignatano.

"You shouldn't be riding around a golf course anyway," Mauch tells Pignatano.

The trainer turns to Walker. "How about it, Rube? I'll put you down. You can ask your wife when you see her."

"Okay," says Walker.

"And I had to pay $10 in greens fees," says Pignatano.

5:10 p.m.

Ed Charles starts dressing for the game. The third baseman—"Pops" to his Met teammates—spent the afternoon in Smithtown, Long Island, showing Little Leaguers the fundamentals of baseball.

"They ask if the Mets are going to win the pennant," says Charles. "I tell them, 'Yep.' You don't want to spoil anything for them. In here, to the writers, I wouldn't talk like that. Only for them."

5:40 p.m.

Rod Gaspar, a rookie outfielder with the Mets, figures he has a chance to play today, because a left-handed pitcher, Ken

Holtzman, will be starting for Chicago. Against all kinds of pitching, Cleon Jones and Tommie Agee, both right-handed hitters, start in left field and center field. Against right-handed pitchers, Art Shamsky, a left-handed hitter, starts in right field. Gil Hodges, who generally manages by the book, accepts the theory that left-handed batters have an edge against right-handed pitchers, and vice versa. Shamsky, even though he is batting .330 on a part-time basis, does not start against left-handed pitchers; instead, Hodges sometimes uses Ron Swoboda, a right-handed swinger, and sometimes Rod Gaspar, a switch-hitter.

Gaspar, twenty-two years old, and Amos Otis, another outfielder, were the most prominent Met rookies during spring training. One or the other was acclaimed each day as the new Mickey Mantle or the new Willie Mays or, at worst, the new Cleon Jones. The attention made Otis, a shy, twenty-one-year-old Alabaman, so nervous he froze when the season started. The Mets shipped him south to Tidewater, Virginia, to thaw out.

Gaspar started the season impressively. In the first two games, he collected four hits, three walks, three stolen bases and an instant fan club. "I like to run," he said. "I wouldn't mind if I was allowed to steal on my own."

But Gaspar couldn't steal first base, and once pitchers around the league learned he had trouble hitting breaking pitches, his batting average plummeted. It is now down to .224, but he is still outhitting his chief rival. Ron Swoboda is batting twenty-two points below his lifetime average of .245, which is still at least twenty-two points below respectabillity.

Gaspar is by far the better defensive man of the two—he has already thrown out seven baserunners this season; once, he caught Lou Brock, the swift St. Louis Cardinal, at the plate to protect a 1–0 Met victory—and now, as he steps out of the runway and into the dugout, he hopes he will be starting against the Cubs.

He walks to the section of the dugout where Gil Hodges has posted the Met lineup and glances down the list. "Dammit," Gaspar mutters. "How the hell do you figure that?" Then he walks to the end of the bench and picks out a seat.

5:45 p.m.

More than two hours before game time, the entire parking lot at Shea Stadium is filled. There hasn't been so much excite-

ment about a baseball game in New York in at least five years,
not since the last time the other New York team played in a
World Series.

6:10 p.m.

Ken Boswell, despite his pop-fly double yesterday, knows he
won't be in the starting lineup. He is a left-handed hitter,
for one thing, and he has a painfully bruised hand. Even when
his hand is healthy, it sometimes hurts—the Mets. Boswell is
in the Met tradition of ironhanded second basemen; he's no
Rod Kanehl, the height of fielding absurdity at second base, but
he's no wizard, no Charlie Gehringer, either. Now, raising his
left hand, Boswell strikes it with his right.

"Ting! Ting!" he says, cocking his ear. "It's a tuning fork.
Ting! Ting!"

6:20 p.m.

Leo Durocher sits in the visiting manager's office playing gin
rummy with an old friend, Barney Kremenko, once a sportswriter for the *New York Journal-American* and now a sports
publicity man.

Joe Reichler, an assistant to the Commissioner of Baseball,
tries to convince Durocher to come out and meet the press.
Durocher says he'd love to, but he has to continue the gin
game with Kremenko. Suddenly, a small boy in a checkered
shirt and sneakers barges into the manager's office.

"How the hell did you get in here?" Durocher says.

"I just walked in," says the boy. He hands the manager a
scorecard and asks for an autograph. Durocher has always
preached and admired nerve. He takes the program and signs it.

"Have you got any old baseballs?" the boy asks.

Durocher's admiration has limits. He points to the door,
and reluctantly, the youngster leaves. "Deal," says Durocher.

As he plays, Durocher starts talking about a recent run-in
between Willie Mays and Clyde King, the manager of the
San Francisco Giants. King is in his first year of managing the
Giants; Durocher ran the club for eight seasons and ran Mays
for four.

"Anybody who tries to manage Willie is crazy," says Durocher. "You don't manage Mays. You just put him in the lineup every day and let him play. When I wanted to say something
to him about something he'd done wrong in the field, I never
took a smile off my face while I was talking."

The mention of Mays reminds Durocher of one of his star pitchers with the Giants, Sal Maglie. "When I went to the mound," Durocher remembers, "I used to call Maglie everything I could think of and get him so mad the veins on his neck would bulge."

Once, Durocher remembers, after he had launched a particularly abusive attack on Maglie's Italian background, the pitcher worked out of a tough situation on the mound, then marched into the dugout. Maglie went directly to the water fountain, picked up a mouthful of water and spat it on the manager's shoes, "He asked me, 'How does it feel?'" Durocher recalls. "I didn't care. I knew I had aroused him and he was ready to pitch."

Reichler makes another try at getting Durocher and the press together, but the manager is still tied up in his gin game. Reichler changes the subject and tries to sign the manager for a post-season tour of the hospitals in Vietnam.

Durocher dismisses him with a grunt—and an anecdote. "One day," he says, "they asked me to a father-and-son dinner in Hackensack and they asked me to bring Willie Mays along. I told Willie I would pick him up at his apartment up there on Coogan's Bluff. Well, I get there and a crowd of about 100 or 150 people gathers. Willie walks out to my car, jumps in the back seat and tells me to drive on. How do you like that?

"And at the dinner, a small boy asks Mays, 'Who is the greatest center fielder?' Well, I hear this and I get the boy up to the dais to repeat the question over the P.A. system. Willie stared at the kid for a minute and then said, 'You're looking at him.'"

Durocher is back in New York, the New York of his Giants and Dodgers.

7:10 p.m.

After a brief team meeting in which Ron Santo apologizes for criticizing Don Young, Leo Durocher finally consents to meet reporters.

"I didn't ask Young what happened on those fly balls. I never criticize a kid for making a bad play in the field," Durocher says, all innocence. "Don's still my center fielder against left-handed pitchers."

His center fielder against right-handed pitchers—Tom Seaver, for instance—is Jim Qualls, a slight, baby-faced rookie. Qualls, at twenty-two, recently returned from three weeks at

Tacoma in the Pacific Coast League and two weeks with his reserve unit in Stockton, California. Of all the Mets, only Bobby Pfeil has ever seen Qualls play, and he hasn't seen him in four years. Pfeil recommends that Seaver throw Qualls "hard stuff"—fast balls and sliders—not curves or change-ups. "He can get his bat on the ball," Pfeil tells Seaver.

7:30 p.m.

In the Met clubhouse, Yogi Berra and Eddie Yost are waiting for Rube Walker. Infield practice starts in five minutes. At the last moment, Walker bursts into the clubhouse and chugs his way toward the field.

As Walker lumbers out, Joe Pignatano, who has been watching Yost reading the *Daily News,* yells to him, "I got you a date for the fan club room."

"Thanks a lot, buddy," replies Yost. He starts flipping through the pages of *Sports Illustrated* until a picture of Oakland's Reggie Jackson catches his eye.

"He's a pretty good ballplayer, huh?" says Yost.

Tom Seaver walks by. "Not built as well as Jones and Agee," says the pitcher.

Yost's arms and face are a deep red from the sun. "I cut the hedges and mowed the lawn today," he says. "It mounts up when you're on the road all the time. I get back from a trip and it's time to mow it again."

7:35 p.m.

The man escorting Mrs. Leo Durocher wears a dark sports jacket and slacks. He is tall, powerfully muscled. His gimlet eyes are deep set, cold, passionless. His broad face seems hewn in granite, a wide mouth slashing across it. Burt Lancaster takes his seat behind the Cub dugout. "I'm an old Met fan," he says. "After all, I'm a native New Yorker. But tonight I'm here as a guest of Leo Durocher so I'll be cheering for the Cubs—and pulling for the Mets. I have to cheer for the Cubs. Otherwise my life would be in danger."

Ernie Banks pops out of the dugout and shakes Lancaster's hand. "Beautiful," says Banks. "Beautiful."

7:38 p.m.

Nick Torman, the Mets clubhouse man, sits in front of Yogi Berra's locker imitating Berra's thick speech. "Hey," says Torman, "Gemme some Kools."

Berra laughs and taps Yost on the shoulder. "Hey," Berra yells, pointing at Torman, "Look at *that!*"

7:40 p.m.

Herb Scharfman, a photographer for *Sports Illustrated*, leans against the wall in Gil Hodges' office, taking pictures of the manager every few seconds.

"Herbie," says Hodges. "I don't believe there's any film in there." Hodges takes off his cap and rubs a big paw through his wavy brown hair. He is almost yawning.

"Aw, Gil," says Scharfman. "I like to take your picture."

George Vecsey, from the *Times*, is watching the photo session. "Herbie," he says, "you've been spending your whole life taking pictures of Gil Hodges."

"I'll tell you something," says Scharfman, in his thick Brooklyn accent. "It's been a pleasure."

7:48 p.m.

Tom Seaver begins warming up with catcher J. C. Martin as Rube Walker looks on. Seaver has the ideal build for a pitcher. A skinny kid until he graduated from high school, he is now as broad around the shoulders as a fullback, yet his muscles are long and loose. Like Robin Roberts, the masterful Philadelphia pitcher of the 1950s to whom he is often compared, Seaver has a smooth, well-controlled delivery. He moves forcefully off his pivot foot, but does not sway.

"We teach our pitchers to keep their butts up straight," says Rube Walker. "We don't want 'em falling back or lunging forward. We want 'em to explode, to push off the mound and deliver the ball in the same continuous motion."

Seaver is having trouble getting loose. His shoulder feels stiff and he can't seem to work it out. He throws 103 warm-up pitches, well beyond what he normally needs to get ready.

"It still feels a little stiff," he says to Walker.

"Do the best you can," says the coach.

8:00 p.m.

Lavonne Koosman drives into the team parking lot behind the Met bullpen. A special duty policeman recognizes her Pontiac Bonneville and opens the gate. A herd of youngsters, perhaps fifty of them, stampede past the policeman as Mrs.

Koosman drives in. They dash towards a nearby gate and disappear under it into the park.

"This is the first time in three years I've had this happen to me," moans the policeman whose hands are cut and bruised from trying to hold the gate closed. "If they win the pennant, I don't know how we'll control this raving mob."

8:02 p.m.

The stadium is packed so tightly the Thin Man couldn't find standing room. Some of the fans lined up as early as 7:30 in the morning to buy their reserved seats. Hundreds of them in general admission seats have been at the park for more than four hours. Hundreds more, who know they can't possibly get tickets, are still standing in lines stretching back to the stairs leading to the elevated subway. On the stairs, dozens more, some with transistor radios, stare at the only part of the field they can see, a slice of green outfield.

The standing room behind home plate is crowded seven deep. Four teenagers from New Jersey vault on top of the telephone booths in back of the standees. The guards leave them alone. There is nowhere else to put them. The total attendance—59,083—is the largest in Met history; so is the tension.

8:04 p.m.

Tom Seaver, throwing his final warm-ups on the mound, feels the stiffness ease in his shoulder. His pitches are going right where he wants them. He is throwing easily.

8:06 p.m.

In the first inning, Tom Seaver retires the Cubs, one-two-three.

8:12 p.m.

Ken Holtzman takes the mound for the Cubs. A tall, slim lefthander with a strong fast ball and a good curve, Holtzman was 9–0 in 1967, then slipped to 11–14 last year. Early this year, he again won nine in a row. But in the last three weeks, Holtzman has not won a game. He has lost three straight.

Tommie Agee hits Holtzman's first pitch inside the right-field line. By the time Al Spangler, playing right field today for the Cubs, can retrieve the ball, Agee is heading toward

64

third base with a triple. The crowd starts chanting, "Let's go, Mets."

Bobby Pfeil hits Holtzman's second pitch into the left-field corner for a double. The Mets lead, 1–0.

As Cleon Jones steps to bat, Ted Abernathy, a thirty-seven-year-old relief pitcher, starts warming up in the bullpen. Time is called while the park policemen clear away half a dozen young fans who climbed the "batter's eye"—the black background placed behind the center-field fence to help batters follow the pitches. "I have been to every ball game here," broadcaster Lindsey Nelson tells the hundreds of thousands of New Yorkers watching the game on television, "and I have never seen anything like this. People are everywhere."

Leo Durocher stands on the dugout steps. His head is down.

Holtzman retires the next three batters, striking out the three and four hitters, Jones and Donn Clendenon. Durocher sits down.

8:27 p.m.

At Tanner Field in Copiague, Long Island, Nelson Burbrink, the director of scouting for the Mets, sits in the stands watching a strong young righthander pitch for a local semi-pro team. Four years ago, Burbrink watched another young righthander pitch for the University of Southern California. His name was Tom Seaver.

Burbrink signed Seaver for the Mets, and ever since, he has compared every prospect to Seaver. Even though the youngster at Tanner Field is still in high school, he measures up pretty well, Burbrink decides. The boy is worth watching. Still, Burbrink would rather be at home, watching Seaver pitch on television.

"I usually watch Tom as much as I can," he says. "I can't say I'm really close to him. I mean, he doesn't come over to the house or anything. But I really sweat it out when he pitches."

8:30 p.m.

In the second inning, Tom Seaver retires the Cubs one-two-three, all on strikeouts.

In the dugout, Rube Walker turns to Gil Hodges. "He's got enough stuff tonight to pitch a no-hitter," says the pitching coach.

8:35 p.m.

With one out in the bottom of the second, Jerry Grote, Tom Seaver's catcher, hits a hard grounder at Ron Santo. The Chicago third baseman blocks it, dances around it and finally picks it up. But by the time his peg reaches first base, on one long bounce, Grote is safe on the error. Al Weis then hits a ground ball toward shortstop. Don Kessinger moves to field the ball, but it seems to pass through his body and out into left-center field.

Seaver comes to bat. At third base, coach Eddie Yost flashes the pitcher the hit sign. Gil Hodges, a conservative manager by nature, normally would ask the pitcher to sacrifice the runners to second and third base. But Ken Holtzman may be unnerved by the poor fielding behind him; Hodges is gambling on a big inning.

Seaver tomahawks a high pitch on a line between first and second base, into right field. Grote scores the second Met run, and Weis moves to third. Then Tommie Agee doubles against the wire fence above the right-field bullpen, and Weis scores easily. Seaver moves to third. The Mets lead, 3–0, and Chicago's Rube Walker walks slowly to the mound.

8:40 p.m.

As Ted Abernathy takes the ride in from the bullpen to replace Ken Holtzman, a chant erupts in the stands behind home plate: "Break up the Mets! Break up the Mets!"

The cry has special meaning for Met fans. On April 23, 1962, when the New York Mets, after nine straight defeats, won the first game in their history, a journeyman catcher named Joe Ginsberg rushed into the Met clubhouse and shouted: "Break up the Mets!" After each of the thirty-nine victories that followed during that season, one ballplayer or another would demand the end of the Met dynasty.

8:48 p.m.

Ted Abernathy, who pitches as though he is skimming rocks across a lake, finishes the inning without further scoring.

8:50 p.m.

On the stage of the Palm Shore Club in Brooklyn, comedian Jack Wakefield is going through his routine. At a front table, pressing his ear to a transistor radio, sits a friend of Wakefield's, David Frisher, a detective with the Queens District Attorney's office. As the third inning ends, Frisher signals Wakefield, raising three fingers on one hand and shaping a zero with the other. Wakefield catches the score and carries on with his act.

8:50 p.m.

Along the right-field foul pole, a policeman walks down the special row reserved for fans in wheelchairs. He stops, suspiciously eyes a young man dressed in Met orange and blue. He yanks the young man out of his wheelchair.

"Where did you get the wheelchair?" the policeman asks the man who is standing quite easily on both feet.

"I took it from the medical room. I wanted to have a good seat."

The policeman leads the fan to the police room under the stands as other fans boo the officer. There are policemen everywhere—regular police, transit police, special police, plainclothesmen, auxiliary police. Outside, scalpers are getting $5 apiece for standing-room tickets.

8:51 p.m.

In the third inning, Tom Seaver retires the Cubs, one-two-three.

8:55 p.m.

As the inning ends, a young man from Brooklyn, George Hubela, who is in his early twenties, rises triumphantly from his seat in the loge section in back of home plate and displays the Met banner wrapped around his chest. Next to him sit his brothers, Louis, fourteen, and John, thirteen, and a friend, Ralph Vilardi, fourteen, all three waving Cub banners.

"The Mets are the greatest," says George Hubela to his companions. "They're the team that's happening, baby. This is it—the New Breed. Jets and Mets, Mets and Jets. That's it. No other teams. The Mets have already gone all the way. They're there. They're going to the moon, the next flight to the moon."

"It'll never happen," taunts Vilardi. "They're a bunch of stiffs."

"They're Yankee fans who hate the Mets," George Hubela

67

explains about his brothers and their friend. "I drove 'em here and paid for their tickets. And before the game is over, I'm gonna brainwash them into liking them Mets."

The brothers wave their Cub banners defiantly.

"I've already mailed in for tickets for the World Series," says George Hubela.

"It'll never happen," answers Vilardi. "Never happen."

"Just wait," says George Hubela. "I'll be here."

8:58 p.m.

In the fourth inning, Tom Seaver retires the Cubs, one-two-three.

9:07 p.m.

In the Met fourth, with one out, Tom Seaver walks, and Tommie Agee steps up. "He's going to get a homer now," cries George Hubela. "He's got a triple and a double. Now he's gonna get a homer."

"Double play," cries brother Louis.

"Watch this shot," counters George.

Agee sends a short fly ball to left field that Billy Williams grabs easily.

"I'm watching," says Louis.

After a Cub error puts Mets on first and second, Cleon Jones comes to bat. "Watch that scoreboard," cries George Hubela. "It's going out there."

"What a bag of wind," says Louis.

Jones strikes out. George Hubela buries his head in his hands.

"What a banana," says Louis.

9:15 p.m.

In the fifth inning, Tom Seaver retires the Cubs one-two-three.

9:19 p.m.

Louis Hubela gets up from his seat and walks through the aisle waving his Cub banner. "Kill that kid," yells brother George, smiling. "That kid's walking home. Lock him up. He ran away from home."

Suddenly, someone throws a hot dog roll in Louis' face. George gets up quickly and looks up. "Who threw that?" he

68

asks, his eyes searching for a guilty face. "Who threw that?"

"He did it," answers a young man in a windbreaker, pointing to a kid in a sports shirt.

"I didn't do it," says the boy in the sports shirt.

"Why don't you come on over here?" challenges the boy's friend.

George Hubela starts walking towards the boys, but an usher and two special policemen hold him back. He struggles for a minute, then goes back to his seat.

"Some nerve," he mutters as he sits down. "I'm a Met fan and the kids are Cub fans. What's the difference? Imagine throwing something at a kid that age."

Ron Swoboda singles to right field, and Hubela is on his feet again, cheering.

"Watch this one," he tells Louis.

Louis watches Jerry Grote fly meekly to right field.

9:25 p.m.

In the sixth inning, Tom Seaver retires the Cubs, one-two-three, picking up his ninth strikeout.

"Old Seaver's throwing pretty good," says Ed Kranepool. "He's got a perfect game."

The rest of the players in the dugout, traditionalists, say nothing.

9:28 p.m.

At the offices of the Associated Press in the middle of Manhattan, an editor dispatches Ed Schuyler, a baseball writer, to Shea Stadium in case Seaver pitches a perfect game. A year ago, when Seaver was pitching a perfect game against the St. Louis Cardinals, Schuyler was sent to the stadium. As he walked into the press box, with one out in the seventh inning, Orlando Cepeda greeted the writer with a single.

9:30 p.m.

Nelson Burbrink, the Mets' scouting chief, decides he has seen enough of the pitching prospect and climbs into his blue Chevrolet Malibu. He turns the car radio to WJRZ, the Met station.

"Tom Seaver will get quite a hand when he comes up to bat here," Lindsey Nelson is saying. "He's faced eighteen Cubs and retired them all." Burbrink thinks briefly about stopping somewhere along the way to watch the game, but he has a long trip home. He contents himself with listening to the game. As he turns onto the Long Island Expressway, the WJRZ signal starts to fade.

9:35 p.m.

The blonde with the classic California face sitting in the box near first base has been watching the game quietly. Now, without warning, tears come pouring down her cheeks. She blots them with a handkerchief. The pressure of the perfect game is getting to Nancy Seaver.

From the mound, Tom Seaver glances quickly at his wife, then turns to face the first batter of the seventh inning.

9:37 p.m.

Don Kessinger leads off for the Cubs. Tom Seaver throws him a high curve that doesn't break, and Kessinger slices a drive deep down the left-field foul line.

"That's it," Seaver mutters to himself.

But Kessinger has hit a fraction under the ball and it hangs up long enough for Cleon Jones to grab it after a long run.

Glenn Beckert lifts a soft fly to right field, a routine play, but Ron Swoboda is nervous as he moves under the ball. "You know it's a perfect game," he says later. "And you don't want to be the schlepp who fouls it up."

Swoboda catches the ball.

The next Cub batter, Billy Williams, hits a low curve ball straight down into the dirt towards third base. It takes a high hop. Ed Charles waits for it. The ball falls slowly as though filmed in slow motion. Finally, Charles grabs it, stumbles for an instant, recovers and throws the ball on a hard, perfect line to first base. The Cubs are out, one-two-three.

"It was nothing," Charles says later.

9:43 p.m.

Cleon Jones goes to the bat rack. He has struck out twice. Tommie Agee, who studies Jones just as carefully as Jones studies him, has noticed something. "You're not staying down on the ball," Agee tells Jones. "You're pulling away from the plate."

Bobby Pfeil flies out, and Jones steps to the plate. He knows

70

he is scheduled to receive an award on Ralph Kiner's post-game television show.

"Here I am, going on TV," he says to himself, "and I haven't contributed anything."

Ted Abernathy gets two strikes on Jones, and no more, Jones hits the next pitch on a straight line over the left-field wall. The Mets lead, 4–0.

9:51 p.m.

Gil Hodges maneuvers for a stronger defense, sending Rod Gaspar to right field, replacing Ron Swoboda, and Wayne Garrett to second base. Bobby Pfeil shifts from second base to his natural position, third base, replacing Ed Charles. Swoboda and Charles pack up their gloves gratefully as the new men take their positions.

"You go into a game like this," Gaspar says later, "cold and everything, and you're just hoping you can do a job if the ball is hit to you. It's a perfect game. We're going for first place. All the people in the park. It's frightening."

"I hope nobody hits the ball to me," Garrett says to himself. "I don't want to mess this up."

9:53 p.m.

In the eighth inning, Tom Seaver retires the Cubs, one-two-three. In the broadcasting booth above home plate, Bob Murphy, Lindsey Nelson and Ralph Kiner scrupulously obey baseball tradition; none has uttered the terrible word: "No-hitter." But, as Seaver throws a fast ball past Al Spangler to end the inning, Murphy shouts into the microphone: "LADIES AND GENTLEMEN, AFTER EIGHT INNINGS, TOM SEAVER IS WALKING INTO THE DUGOUT WITH A PERFECT BALL GAME." He still didn't say "no-hitter."

9:55 p.m.

With one man on base, Tom Seaver comes to the plate. He stands outside the batter's box, and the roar of the huge, standing crowd sweeps over him.

"I wanted to soak it up," Seaver says later. "If they wanted to give me an ovation like that, I wanted to give them the opportunity to do it."

The cheers rock the stadium for more than a minute. Finally, Seaver steps in and does his job, sacrificing the runner to second. The Mets do not score, and no one particularly cares.

9:57 p.m.

By now, two-and-a-half million television viewers in the New York area are watching Tom Seaver pursue the perfect game. Housewives not the least interested in baseball have been dragged to the set by their husbands to watch history. They see, first, a Chrysler commercial, urging them to "dream the impossible dream."

10:03 p.m.

In a box near the Mets' dugout, the former United States Ambassador to the Court of St. James turns his face away from the field. "I'm chicken," says John Hay Whitney, the brother of the Mets' president, Joan Whitney Payson. "I can't watch this last inning."

Whitney, who has seen only the Met opener and no other 1969 games before this Cub series, considers himself a typical Met fan. "I share the spirit of the 59,000 Met fans here," says Whitney, the amiable multi-millionaire owner of Greentree Stables, the Whitney Communications Corporation, and half a dozen homes. He does not own any share of the Mets.

10:04 p.m.

In a box not far from John Hay Whitney's, Nancy Seaver is still weeping. She has shredded her handkerchief with her fingers. Nearby, Charles Seaver, Tom's father, sits with his fists clenched, his knuckles white.

10:05 p.m.

On the mound, Tom Seaver can feel the adrenalin flowing through his body. His arm is incredibly light, almost detached from his body. He can hear his heart pounding like a jackhammer. He can hear nothing outside his body. The roar of the crowd has temporarily deafened him.

Randy Hundley steps in. Hundley notices that Bobby Pfeil is playing deep at third base. On Seaver's first pitch, a high fast ball, Hundley suddenly turns and bunts—right back to Seaver.

"Take your time!" yells catcher Jerry Grote. "Take your time!"

Seaver takes his time and throws Hundley out.

10:06 p.m.

At a small restaurant called Giovanni's in Watertown, a slim young sergeant is standing before the television set, his fists clenched, cheering Seaver on.

"Who in the hell is that guy?" asks a voice from the back of the restaurant. "Is he drunk?"

Bud Harrelson, the Met shortstop and Tom Seaver's roommate when he isn't on military training, doesn't turn around to see who yelled. His eyes are fixed on the television set.

10:07 p.m.

Jimmy Qualls comes to bat. A left-handed hitter, Qualls has been to bat in the major leagues only forty-seven times. He is hitting .243. In center field, Tommie Agee thinks for a moment of moving a few steps toward left field. Then he recalls that Qualls has pulled the ball sharply his first two times up; the first time, he hit a line drive off a fast ball—Tom Seaver's "hard stuff"—that backed Ron Swoboda to the right-field wall.

"If anyone's going to break it up," Agee says to himself, "it's this guy." Behind the plate, Jerry Grote calls for more hard stuff—the fast ball. Seaver nods.

10:08 p.m.

Ed Schuyler, the Associated Press writer, rushes up the runway at Shea Stadium and into the press box.

10:08 p.m.

Tom Seaver throws to Jim Qualls. The fast ball is waist-high, almost over the heart of the plate. Qualls swings and connects and the ball carries deep to left-center field. Tommie Agee breaks after the ball. He looks quickly at Cleon Jones. Jones shakes his head. As the two outfielders converge, the ball falls safely between them.

10:08 p.m.

At Giovanni's in Watertown, Bud Harrelson watches Qualls' line drive fall and swears at the television set.

10:08 p.m.

On the Long Island Expressway Nelson Burbrink, straining to pick up the play-by-play from Shea Stadium, hears that Jimmy Qualls has singled. He swears at the radio.

10:09 p.m.

All the adrenalin that has been pumping through Tom Seaver suddenly drains out of his body. He stands on the mound with his glove hand resting on his hip and stares into left-center field. Then he puts his head down. The crowd which has booed Jimmy Qualls is now standing, cheering, screaming for Seaver.

Seaver is numb. "It was within my grasp," he says later. "I could have had it. You just don't get another chance. I can't measure the disappointment."

Donn Clendenon comes over from first base to steady Seaver. "Don't let down," he says. "Let's get the last two outs."

Al Weis stands near second base. While playing for the White Sox, he once watched Joel Horlen pitch a no-hitter for eight and one-third innings against Washington. Then Horlen gave up a single, then a home run and lost, 2–1.

"Let's get this game over with," Weis says to himself. He yells to Seaver, "I'll be covering second on anything hit back to you."

10:10 p.m.

Tom Seaver goes back to work, and, with no trouble at all, retires the Cubs, two-three. There is little excitement on the field. The players gather around the pitcher, shaking his hand as they do with all winning pitchers. But the scene looks more like a condolence call than a celebration. Seaver disappears into the dugout. The crowd chants, "We want Seaver," but he is too far away to hear them.

10:14 p.m.

Outside the studio where the post-game show is telecast, Nancy Seaver stands with teary red eyes. Tom Seaver spots her as he comes down the hall. "What are you crying for?" he asks. "We won, 4–0."

74

Nancy smiles. "I guess a one-hit shutout is better than nothing," she says.

Tom Seaver smiles, too.

10:16 p.m.

Rod Gaspar trots into the Met clubhouse. "How come you're sweating?" someone asks him. "You didn't even make a play."

10:18 p.m.

Sitting in front of their lockers, Jerry Grote and Al Weis gently question the night's official scorer, Steve Jacobson, a writer for *Newsday,* about his judgment in giving Ron Santo and Don Kessinger errors on hard-hit ground balls early in the game.

"The players don't worry much when you give *them* errors," says Jacobson who, like all official scorers, gets a fee of $30 a game. "What bothers them is when you call a ball they hit an error rather than a base hit. That's what you'll hear about after the game."

Ed Kranepool comes over to Jacobson and starts chewing him out about a ball he hit on June 27 that the scorer called an error.

"You'll see," Kranepool growls. "I'm going to screw you writers out of that money for scoring."

10:19 p.m.

The Met clubhouse is quiet, subdued, letdown, almost as if they had lost.

10:20 p.m.

The Cub clubhouse is also quiet, except for the manager. "Nobody was going to beat Seaver tonight," Leo Durocher says. "I never saw him throw so hard. If he keeps throwing that hard, nobody's going to beat him. But I don't think he will.

"We're still three games ahead. And from now on the Mets are going to find the going rougher. They're going to see the best pitchers in the league."

Durocher smiles at the reporters around him. "That Qualls ruined you guys," he says. "He made you rewrite your stories."

Nearby, Jimmy Qualls is talking to another pack of reporters. "There was no pressure on me at all," the rookie says. "All I wanted to do was get a base hit and get something started."

Was Qualls thinking of breaking up the perfect game?

"I wasn't thinking of anything but of going to the plate and getting a hit so we could win the game," he says. "He gave me a waist-high fast ball. When they give you a good pitch, you've got to hit it."

At twenty-two, Qualls has already mastered the baseball lexicon.

10:21 p.m.

On the post-game TV show, with Tom Seaver, Nancy Seaver and Cleon Jones as his guests, Ralph Kiner introduces the replay of Jim Qualls' base hit. "He hit the ball well," says Kiner, "so at least you won't go home and say it was lucky."

"He's a sticky little hitter," says Seaver.

Kiner turns to Cleon Jones. "Cleon," he says, "I guess you're going to take over this show, you've been on it so often."

"Well, Ralph," says Jones, easily, "I'll give you another year. I'll give you this year. I'll take over next year."

10:29 p.m.

Tom Seaver goes back to the Met clubhouse. Chicago's Dick Selma, the ex-Met who grew up with Seaver in Fresno, California, comes bouncing in, goes over to Seaver and slaps him on the back.

"Who were you pulling for?" Seaver says, laughing.

"I was pulling for us," says Selma.

10:30 p.m.

Ed Kranepool turns to a reporter. "It would be great," he says, "to go into Chicago the last two games of the season with a three-game lead and tell Ernie Banks, 'It's a great day to play two, Ernie.' "

10:32 p.m.

The other New York team loses in extra innings and falls twenty and a half games out of first place.

10:35 p.m.

Billy Williams visits his fellow Alabamans, Cleon Jones and Tommie Agee, in the Met clubhouse. "The man just pitched a one-hitter," says Williams. "That's all. Just another one-hitter."

CUBS vs METS at SHEA STADIUM DATE JULY 9, 1969

PLAYER	Pos	1	2	3	4	5	6	7	8	9	10	11	12	AB	R	H	SB	SO	BB	PO	A	E	
KESSINGER	6													4	0	0	0	0	0	2	3	1	2 base hits.
BECKERT	4													3	0	0	0	0	1	3	3	0	3 base hits.
WILLIAMS	7													3	0	0	0	1	0	3	0	0	Home runs -
SANTO	5													3	0	0	0	0	0	0	3	1	Double plays.
BANKS	3													3	0	0	0	0	2	9	0	0	Left on bases, with HOLTZMAN-0 ABERNATHY-2
SPANGLER	9													3	0	0	0	0	3	0	0	0	Struck out by HOLTZMAN-2 ABERNATHY-2
HUNDLEY	2													3	0	0	0	0	4	0	1	0	Bases on balls, off HOLTZMAN-1½ ABERNATHY-6⅔ Earned runs off HOLTZMAN-4 ABERNATHY-1
QUALLS	8													2	0	1	0	0	3	0	0	0	Winning pitcher SEAVER (N-3)
ABERNATHY	1													1	0	0	0	0	0	2	0	0	Losing pitcher HOLTZMAN (20-8)
HOLTZMAN	1													0	0	0	0	0	0	1	0	0	Umpires.
SMITH ph														1	0	0	0	0	0	0	0	0	
																							Attendance.
																							Score.
TOTALS		0	0	0	0	0	0	0	0	0				28	0	1	0	1	24	9	13		Time of game 2:02

METS vs CUBS at SHEA STADIUM DATE JULY 9, 1969

PLAYER		1	2	3	4	5	6	7	8	9	10	11	12	AB	R	H	BB	SO	SB	SO	PO	A	E
AGEE	8													5	1	2	0	1	0	0	2	0	0
PFEIL	4													4	0	1	0	1	0	0	0	0	0
JONES	7													3	1	1	1	0	2	0	3	0	0
CLENDENON	3													4	0	0	0	0	0	1	6	0	0
GARRETT—9th	4													0	0	0	0	0	0	1	0	0	0
CHARLES	5													4	0	1	0	0	0	1	1	4	0
GASPAR—9th	9													0	0	0	0	0	0	2	0	0	0
SWOBODA	9													4	0	1	0	0	0	2	0	0	0
GROTE	2													4	1	0	0	0	0	0	11	0	0
WEISS	6													4	1	1	0	0	0	0	0	1	0
SEAVER	1													2	0	1	1	0	1	1	0	1	0
TOTALS														34	4	8	2	4	0	4	27	6	0

1 base on PFEIL, AGEE, CHARLES
2 base on AGEE
Home run JONES
Double play
Runs batted in GRANTE—0
Struck out by SEAVER—11
Innings pitch by SEAVER—9
Earned run off SEAVER—0
Opponent hits off SEAVER—0
Wild pitches
Balks
Passed balls
Winning pitcher SEAVER (14-3)
Losing pitcher HOLTZMAN (9-5)
Umpires PELEKOUDAS, VARGO, DEZELAN, CRAWFORD
Scorer
Time of game 2:02

Three

The Day The Mets Relapsed

THURSDAY
JULY 10, 1969

NATIONAL LEAGUE STANDINGS
Eastern Division

	W	L	PCT.	G.B.
Chicago	52	33	.612	–
New York	47	34	.580	3
Pittsburgh	41	43	.488	10½
St. Louis	42	45	.483	11
Philadelphia	37	45	.451	13½
Montreal	26	58	.310	25½

On July 10, 1966, when the New York Mets took the field against the Pittsburgh Pirates, they knew they had a good chance to set a major-league record. If they could avoid beating the Pirates, they would become the first team in baseball history to lose 500 games in its first five seasons.

The Mets had the odds going for them. During their first four seasons, they had managed to underscore the Pirates four out of every five times the teams met; during their first four seasons, they had never outscored anyone on July 10.

Yet for seven and a half innings, the Mets held the Pirates even, 4–4. Then, in the bottom of the eighth inning, Pittsburgh came up with five straight hits, Chuck Hiller—"Dr. No"— contributed his specialty, a misplayed ground ball, and the Mets clinched an historic 9–4 defeat.

Still, the Mets could not really complain. The defeat was only their forty-eighth in eighty-three games; never before had they gone through so many games of a season with so few defeats. And, at the end of the day, they led the Chicago Cubs by nine full games and, for the first time on this date, trailed only eight other National League teams.

Since the defeat in Pittsburgh in 1966, the Mets have never lost a game on July 10. The explanation is simple: Thanks to the annual All-Star Game break, the Mets, in 1967 and 1968, did not play on July 10.

12:20 a.m.

More than two hours after Tom Seaver's imperfect game, Shea Stadium police are still chasing some one hundred teen-agers who are running across the outfield and hiding in the stands and in the corners of the ball park. Many of the young-sters have infiltrated through a large hole cut into a wire fence near the bullpen.

Larry Janof, a special guard who wears badge #69, is among the officers chasing the kids. "At night, with the tunnels and the doors unlocked and unguarded," he says, "you can't see everyone. We're having a hell of a time."

Finally, at 12:45, the officers manage to clear the teenagers from Shea Stadium. A few writers remain, pounding out their stories of Seaver's victory for the afternoon newspapers.

12:50 a.m.

At his apartment high in the Waldorf Towers, Frank Sinatra is entertaining a friend, Leo Durocher. The sixty-two-year-old

Chicago manager is recovering both from a party Sinatra gave in his honor the other night at Jilly's a "Rat Pack" hangout, and from the Cubs' fifth straight defeat.

A friend of Durocher's, a man who saw Don Larsen pitch a perfect game against the Dodgers in the 1956 World Series and saw Jim Bunning pitch a perfect game against the Mets in 1964, asks Durocher how he feels about Jim Qualls' single, the hit that spoiled Tom Seaver's perfect game. "Tell me the truth," the friend says to Durocher. "You knew you weren't going to win it. Aren't you a little bit sorry that your man got the hit?"

Durocher leans over and whispers, "Go love yourself."

3:40 a.m.

In the press room at Shea Stadium, a Western Union operator files the last of 40,300 words, a Met record for a single game.

6:15 a.m.

In his crib in Elmhurst, Long Island, Chris Gentry is running a fever, the result of a measles shot the eleven-month-old baby received a few days ago. He starts to howl, waking his father, Gary Gentry, for the sixth time in eight hours. Gentry rolls over and tries to go back to sleep. His wife, Janet, gets up and quiets Chris. Gary Gentry, a rookie pitcher for the Mets, is scheduled to face the Cubs this afternoon.

9:30 a.m.

Eddie Yost leaves his home in Hauppauge, Long Island, for Shea Stadium. As the Met coach walks to his car, his five-year-old son, Michael, runs to the door.

"Nice baseball, Daddy," he says.

9:45 a.m.

Ken Boswell, the Met infielder who is leaving for a weekend of military reserve duty after today's game, gobbles down his breakfast—a peanut-butter-and-jam sandwich. "I'm not a breakfast eater," says Boswell. "I hate eggs." He shakes his head. "I don't see how anybody can get so excited about something that comes out of a chicken's butt," he says.

82

9:55 a.m.

On the way out to the park, Ed Charles of the Mets stops at a stationery store to pick up a newspaper. "Way to go," a man in the store tells him. "Keep it up."

Charles hasn't done much for the Mets this season. The club's leader in home runs in 1968, he has hit only two this year and his average is an even .200. But to Met fans today, after two straight stirring victories over the Cubs, every Met is a hero, even a fading, part-time, thirty-six-year-old third baseman.

10:15 a.m.

John V. Lindsay, the Mayor of New York, stands in front of City Hall in downtown Manhattan, inspecting the interior of a new subway car. Newsmen crowd around him to hear his reaction to the new piece of equipment. He starts talking about the car, then shifts the subject. "I don't know what could be more exciting than the victory of the Mets," he says. "Perhaps that's what we ought to be talking about."

The Mayor finishes his inspection of the subway car and walks back to his office. He places a telephone call. "Hello," he says. "Gil Hodges? This is John Lindsay. Tell Leo that Chicago is still the second city. We're bursting with pride over the Mets. I know it's an uphill fight and I think I know something about uphill fights. Let's go, Mets!"

Lindsay places a second call, to Tom Seaver. "Your fantastic pitching is giving you an unbelievable year," says the Mayor, who is basically a football fan. "I'm just sorry you lost the perfecto last night. But it was a great job. Let's go all the way, the pennant and then the Series."

The Mets are fighting for a pennant, and John V. Lindsay is fighting for re-election. Neither is expected to win.

11:05 a.m.

At Davidow & Co., a Manhattan manufacturer of women's suits, the busy season is in full swing. Steven Davidow, the company's vice-president, sits at his desk. "We're swamped with orders," Davidow says to a visitor. "I'll be stuck at this desk all day."

11:15 a.m.

Gary Gentry sits by his locker at Shea Stadium. Despite his restless night, he does not feel tired. "I'm not one of these guys who needs a certain amount of rest every night," he says. "But I can feel when I need it. For instance, in Philadelphia once, we got into town late. I went to sleep at midnight and woke up at noon, got something to eat and went back to sleep for two or three more hours. Then I pitched my best game of the year."

Gentry has the same kind of immobile face as Buster Keaton. His stone stare rarely changes. But beneath this reserved facade, he is a confident, aggressive pitcher.

He has been in organized baseball only two years. During his first season, at Williamsport in the Eastern League, Whitey Herzog, the Mets' director of player development, called him "one of the three best prospects in the minors."

The young righthander didn't argue. "I pitched at junior college and at Arizona State against the best competition," he says. "And I had a good year at Jacksonville. There's no way I could learn any more about pitching by being in the minors. No way. This is where the best hitters are and this is where I'm gonna pitch—and win."

Gentry has been winning. His record is 8–6. "Listen," he says. "If you don't know what you can do at twenty-two, you never will."

The rookie pitcher slips into his uniform. Six feet tall and 175 pounds, Gentry is so slender the word "Mets" sits low on his chest and the pinstripes wrinkle. The shoulder lines fall down around his biceps.

"Nervous?" a reporter asks.

"Not in the least," Gentry says, stifling a yawn. "Today's like any other day that I'm pitching as far as I'm concerned."

11:30 a.m.

Steven Davidow, the vice-president of Davidow & Co., hails a cab on the corner of Seventh Avenue and 39th Street.

"Where to?" says the driver.

"Shea Stadium," says Davidow.

12:15 p.m.

Ed Charles sits by his locker. "Too damn close not to get that," he says, referring to Tom Seaver's lost bid for a perfect game

84

last night. Charles himself lost a double when Jimmy Qualls made a shoestring catch of his line drive.

Nick Torman, the Mets' clubhouse man, delivers a telegram to Charles: YOU AND SEAVER WERE ROBBED BY QUALLS. GOOD LUCK TODAY.

12:20 p.m.

Larry Merchant, a sports columnist for the *New York Post*, brings a tape recorder into the middle of the clubhouse. He is wearing a blinding orange and yellow floral sports jacket.

Ron Swoboda gazes at the jacket in disbelief. "Is that a record?" he asks Merchant.

"No," says Merchant, looking down at the jacket. "But it ties the record."

Swoboda laughs. Merchant's remark reminds the outfielder of a line from *Hombre*, a Paul Newman movie.

"This other guy has a shotgun trained on Newman," says Swoboda, training an imaginary shotgun on Merchant. "Newman is about to draw. Then he stops and says, 'Remember, if you tie me, you're dead.' "

12:35 p.m.

Leo Durocher sits in his office, flatly refusing all television and radio interviews. He has nothing against those media. He just limits his appearances to his favorite show, his own, a pre-game radio show carried in Chicago.

Today Durocher is entertaining a few New York newspapermen with variations on a familiar Cub theme—downgrading the Mets. "There's no way the Mets can go on this way," he says. "We won a few games and were eight games ahead of everybody. Then we came back down, and they will, too. Just wait and see."

Eventually, as always with the New York writers, Durocher turns to the past, to Don Mueller, a precise and reliable outfielder who played for the New York Giants in the early 1950s.

"Mueller had a funny way of moving about," recalls Leo. "It was the way he ran. There was one club—I can't remember which one—that always got on Mueller and called him half-man, half-woman. This used to bother the hell out of me. I told Don that I'd give him $500 if he'd go back at those guys and challenge them to come out of the dugout and repeat it. But he never did.

"I told him all the time about this $500 in my locker just waiting for him, but what they said never seemed to bother Mueller. Why, if they'd said that to me, I'd have gone out there. I wouldn't have cared how big the guys were. I might've ended up with them jumping on my head, but I just wouldn't have taken it."

To prove his point, Leo tells how he and Frankie Frisch collaborated at shortstop and second base for the Giants in the 1930s. "When there was a man on first base," Leo says, "I'd tell Frisch to take the ball for the tag on a double play and I'd go over there and stomp all over the runner. When the guy complained, I'd just smile and tell him I was trying to get out of the way. The guy never believed me, though."

12:50 p.m.

Billy Williams roams about the batting cage. In the box seats nearby, a tall, dark-haired girl with long hair and bell-bottom trousers watches Williams' every movement. Williams hits three quick ones and moves out of the cage. The girl is still staring.

Williams looks over his bat, moves around the cage and turns out to the field. The girl doesn't take her eyes off him. Finally, Williams raises his hand in the victory sign. The girl jumps up and down, waving and shouting. Williams doesn't know her. He just laughs and goes back into the cage.

1:40 p.m.

Coach Rube Walker is hitting infield practice for the Mets for the eighth straight day. Coach Yogi Berra grabs a glove and goes out to play first base.

Bobby Pfeil, from third base, throws a ball low, into the dirt. Berra bends, but the ball skips by him and ricochets into the dugout. Coach Joe Pignatano ducks behind the ball bag for survival. "Hey, hey, hey, Yogi!" Pignatano yells. "Beautiful! Beautiful!"

1:45 p.m.

Gary Gentry warms up in the bullpen. His arm almost takes his ear off as he delivers his fast ball, his best pitch, straight overhand. He can throw a change of pace, but he isn't convinced that he should. "Mr. Wes Stock and Mr. Rube Walker, they taught me the pitch," Gentry says. "They told me I should use it. I had a pretty good one in winter ball. I'll use it when they call for it, but there's no way I'd throw it on my own."

After throwing ninety-three pitches, Gentry tells Walker, "I feel fine. Let's go get 'em."

1:50 p.m.

In the Met dugout, Rube Walker and Gary Gentry sit side by side, neither saying a word.

"Did you give Gentry any briefing?" a reporter asks Walker.

The Mets' pitching coach glances at the Mets' rookie pitcher. "Hell, no," says Walker, grinning. "The manager told me to stay away from the pitchers. I might louse them up."

1:55 p.m.

The vice-president of the Valley National Bank in Glendale, California, accepts a person-to-person call from Phil Pepe, a sportswriter for the *New York News*. Pepe would like to hear the banker's opinion of the new Mets; the banker is qualified, partly because he is also a vice-president of the Mets, mostly because he is Charles Dillon Stengel.

"Eighty-five people have called me up," says Casey Stengel, as precise as ever. He is the man who became the Mets' first manager in 1962; from 1949 through 1960, he won ten pennants and seven world championships managing the New York Yankees, a record which did nothing to prepare him for the Mets. He accepted his fall from the sublime to the ridiculous with good humor and labeled the Mets "Amazin'." Although his four years in last place ruined his lifetime managerial average, the seventy-eight-year-old banker still looks upon the Mets with grandfatherly affection. "They're doin' wonderful," he says, "beatin' the big fellers. I'll be stayin' back here pullin' for that team to win and win and win."

And Casey is off, running his rhetorical obstacle course. "They're beatin' Chicago and everybody thought that was a strong club and the only time that club is weakenin' is now," he says. "When you commence to beat the big fellers, you're gettin' good and that really shocked the people because they can't believe it. But when you beat them it means two games and I know because I was in a number of pennant races and I win it.

"Like I said, they are the Amazin' Mets. They're really hot-shots now, hot potatoes. I ain't made plans as far ahead as

October yet, but that's only 'cause Mrs. Payson has so many friends that I don't like to call her and ask her for 100 tickets."

2:00 p.m.

Ernie Banks, the cheerful Cub, stares toward the New York dugout. "Look at those Mets," he says. "They're calm for such a young team. That's pretty strange."

2:03 p.m.

Bill Hands, the starting Chicago pitcher, settles into the Cub dugout. He does not have overpowering speed, but his control and his breaking pitches—which lend his fast ball the element of surprise—make him a tough pitcher. The Mets have had trouble hitting him for the past two seasons, they haven't beaten him since 1967. Hands, says Gil Hodges, the New York manager, "has a hook" in the Met batters.

2:04 p.m.

Bob Murphy, the starting Met broadcaster on New York's Channel 9 today, goes down the lineups of the two clubs, flavoring his words with straight televese. Gary Gentry is the "tall, slender rookie righthander from Phoenix, Arizona"; Tommie Agee has "awesome power"; Wayne Garrett is "the Huckleberry Finn of the New York Mets." Murphy, who used to work for the Boston Red Sox, is a master of the English language, sports division. Long fly balls that might go foul "have the legs" to be home runs. The oldest umpire on the field is, invariably, "the senior arbiter of the umpiring crew." Every Oldtimer's Day brings back to Shea Stadium "a galaxy of stars." Men are always "reaching on a walk" or "reaching on an error," omitting the word "base," as if it were an obscenity. Last night, as the first Cub batter of the ninth inning faced Tom Seaver, Murphy suggested to his audience, "Now listen to the hush falling over this big crowd."

2:05 p.m.

In the first inning, Gary Gentry retires the Cubs, one-two-three.

2:11 p.m.

In the first inning, the Mets' first batter, Tommie Agee, drives Bill Hands' fifth pitch over the right-center field fence.

The Mets lead, 1–0.
Amazing.

2:16 p.m.

In the second inning, Gary Gentry loses his perfect game, with the help of an umpire.

Ron Santo, the Cub third baseman, leads off with a ground ball to third. The play is routine, but umpire Frank Dezelan rules that Ed Kranepool, playing first base for the Mets, lifted his foot off the bag. Kranepool argues with Dezelan, and loses. A television replay, showing Kranepool's foot firmly on the base, indicates that the wrong man won the argument.

As Gentry retires the Cubs on a double play and a pop foul, Joe Pignatano, out in right field, finishes walking his seventh lap around the Met bullpen. "It eases the tension," he says. "I pretend to be looking for something."

2:28 p.m.

In the third inning, Gary Gentry retires the Cubs, one-two-three, protecting his 1–0 lead. Jimmy Qualls, greeted by boos from the Met fans, grounds to shortstop for the middle out. "Too bad he didn't do that last night," says someone in the Met dugout.

2:40 p.m.

In the fourth inning, Gary Gentry loses his no-hitter, his shut-out and all resemblance to Tom Seaver. First he walks Don Kessinger. Then Glenn Beckert lines a single to center field. Billy Williams pops up.

"They invoke the infield fly rule," announces Bob Murphy, invoking the inevitable verb for the infield fly rule.

Ron Santo, the next hitter, hits an inside fast ball deep toward the left-field fence. "That's out of the park," Santo thinks, as he runs toward first.

The ball is out of the park, but Cleon Jones, his back against the fence, leaps, reaches over the fence and pulls the ball back in.

Santo trots back to the dugout. "Things just aren't going right," he says to himself.

2:45 p.m.

With Don Kessinger and Glenn Beckert still on first and second, two out and Ernie Banks at bat, thirty-six Cub fans, bunched together, cheer for a base hit. They are part of a group called the Cub Tour, which will follow the Cubs to Los Angeles, San Francisco and San Diego.

Louis Cernowsky of Fox River Grove, Illinois, sits in the front of the Chicago section with his twelve-year-old grandson, David, who has met all the Cubs and received two autographed baseballs. "We felt terrible after the first game, coming all this way," Cernowsky says. "It was a big disappointment for us. We felt the Cubs had it in the bag. The Mets were lucky."

Banks singles past the shortstop to tie the game, 1–1.

"We needed that," says Cernowsky. "I'm sure the Cubs are going to win this one. No doubt at all."

The next batter pops out to third.

3:03 p.m.

In the bottom of the fourth, with the bases loaded, Ed Kranepool comes through, mildly. He hits a weak ground ball to first, a run scores and the Mets lead once more, 2–1.

3:08 p.m.

A few seats are empty in Shea Stadium, but only a few. There are 49,752 spectators on hand, 36,012 of whom have paid their way into the park. Most of the non-paying guests are Midget Mets, gathered in the upper deck. For the three-game series, the total attendance is 163,931, the paid attendance 123,752. The crowd today makes the Mets the first National League team in 1969 to pass the million mark in paid attendance.

The Mets have always drawn good crowds—roughly a million a year for two seasons in the old Polo Grounds, then never less than a million and a half spectators a season since they moved into Shea Stadium in 1964. But in the early years, the people came to watch comedy, to watch Elio Chacon manhandle a ground ball, to watch Choo Choo Coleman dig a bad pitch out of the dirt and then rifle a throw into center field, to watch Jesse Gonder, who had a better arm, fail to dig a bad pitch out of the dirt, to watch pitchers like Ray Daviault, Jay Hook, Bob G. Miller and Bob L. Miller throw half-speed pitches—never too fast and never too slow—over the center of the plate.

Now the people come to watch drama, to watch Cleon Jones

and Tommie Agee, Tom Seaver and Jerry Koosman, all the new breed, a gifted, alert group of ballplayers.

3:09 p.m.

In the fifth inning, Jimmy Qualls, leading off for the Cubs, lines a base hit into right field. Art Shamsky, lumbering after the ball, allows Qualls to stretch a sure single into a double. Man on second.

The next Cub batter, pitcher Bill Hands, bunts, and Jerry Grote, the Met catcher, fires the ball to third. The Mets catch Qualls in a rundown, but as he retreats to second, Al Weis, the Met shortstop, drops a low throw. Men on first and second.

After Don Kessinger ties up the game with a single, Glenn Beckert bunts. Gentry, the confident twenty-two-year-old rookie, reaches for the ball, misses it and reaches for it again. Bases loaded.

Billy Williams hits a line drive to center field, and Tommie Agee makes the catch perfectly, then, with no chance of getting Hands at the plate, throws home, anyway. The other two Chicago baserunners, Kessinger and Beckert, tag up and start to advance. Catcher Grote grabs Agee's throw and fires to second, attempting to catch Beckert. Ken Boswell, the man with the tuning-fork hand, reaches for Grote's throw and sweeps his gloved hand down to tag Beckert, a graceful play with only one flaw. Boswell has missed the throw. Kessinger trots home, and the Cubs lead, 4–2.

No Met misplays the ball hit by the next batter, Ron Santo. His last time up, Santo had a home run pulled back into the park by Cleon Jones. But Jones would have to be playing Santo shaded toward the top of the upper left-field deck to rob him this time. Gary Gentry's slider doesn't—and Santo drives the ball over the auxiliary scoreboard. The Cubs lead, 6–2.

The huge Met crowd is subdued, almost shocked, more by the Mets' mishaps than by the Chicago rally. Some of the fans don't quite believe what has happened. They have been spoiled by the new breed, a gifted, alert group of ballplayers.

3:22 p.m.

Gil Hodges, the Met manager, heads for the mound, and Gary Gentry knows, immediately, that he is heading for the showers. "Hodges doesn't have to say anything," Gentry says later. "When he comes out there, you know what it's for."

Gentry marches off the field. "I didn't have it," he says. "I was making a lot of bad pitches. They were going mostly down the middle. I wasn't concentrating. I knew this was a big game. I guess I just wasn't ready mentally."

3:25 p.m.

The man who would, under normal circumstances, replace Gary Gentry at this point is not in the Met bullpen. He is sitting in a jeep, stuck in the mud of a North Carolina swamp. "At least I could just throw the jeep into four-wheel drive and get out of it," Tug McGraw, serving two weeks of military duty in the Marine Corps at Camp Lejeune, says later. "Gary couldn't."

McGraw, an aggressive, spirited young man, is the Mets' middle-inning relief pitcher, a traditionally frustrating job. The middle-inning reliever most often appears when the starting pitcher collapses and the opposing team leads by at least a few runs. If he does his job well, he will hold the other team scoreless for a few innings, then be replaced by a pinch-hitter. If he does his job well, and his teammates catch up and win, he will often watch the late-inning reliever get credit for the victory. He gets little attention, and little reward. There have been good middle-inning relief pitchers, and bad ones, but very few rich ones.

McGraw is not yet rich, but he is only twenty-four years old, and he has established himself this year as one of the good middle-inning relievers. Just a week ago, he came into a game against the St. Louis Cardinals with the score tied, 4–4, and the Cardinals charging; he pitched six scoreless innings, and the Mets won in the fourteenth. McGraw's record is 5–1, with five saves to his credit. Until this year, he was known best for achieving the first victory in Met history over the great Dodger lefthander, Sandy Koufax. In 1965, four days before his twenty-first birthday, McGraw beat Koufax, 6–2.

"I really miss the hell out of the Cub series," says McGraw. "I've always pitched well against Chicago." His lifetime record against the Cubs is 2–3.

"Well," he says, "at least this year I've pitched well against them. If it was Montreal or somebody, I wouldn't miss it that much. But it's Chicago, and I'd like to be there. And where am I? Out in the swamps with Captain Cook."

3:28 p.m.

Cal Koonce, once a starting pitcher with the Cubs, now normally a late-inning reliever for the Mets, replaces Gary Gentry, and sets down Chicago without further scoring. The Mets trot off the field, the Cubs trot on and the scoreboard registers nothing.

The scoreboard has broken down, flatly refusing to concede Chicago its five runs and its 6–2 lead. Each of the inning-by-inning scores has burned out. The numbers of some of the Met players have burned out. But Bill Hands hasn't. The Chicago pitcher retires the Mets easily in the fifth inning.

3:47 p.m.

In the seventh inning, with the score still 6–2, a television commercial for Rheingold beer offers Met fans a chance to watch a young hitter who "knocks the cover off the ball." He is a hot hitter in the spring, an announcer explains, but will he still be hitting in the fall? Only time will tell. The youngster must stand up to the test of time, and so must Rheingold, the beer with the ten-minute head. Since the commercial lasts a minute or less, the average viewer has a very difficult time judging whether or not the Rheingold head actually stands up for ten minutes; he doesn't have a very difficult time judging whether the youngster's hitting is going to stand up. His swing is not impressive. In fact, his swing is downright amateurish. The commercial may have been filmed in an early Met training camp.

4:01 p.m.

The scoreboard comes to life in the eighth inning, but the Mets don't. For the fourth straight inning, they go down without a hit. The Cubs still lead, 6–2.

"We just don't have it today," says Barbara Weis, Al Weis's wife, who predicted the Mets' ninth-inning rally Tuesday.

4:26 p.m.

Mrs. Al Weis is right again. In the ninth inning, Bill Hands retires the Mets, one-two-three. Ed Kranepool, the middle out, earns a round of boos.

Sic Transit Gloria Tuesday.

4:30 p.m.

"I predicted that 6–2 score in the third inning," says Louis Cernowsky of the Cub Tour. "And I predict that whoever wins the three games in Chicago next week will win the pennant. The Cardinals are definitely out of the race."

"Jimmy the Greek" Snyder, the Las Vegas oddsmaker, agrees with Louis Cernowsky. He is announcing his mid-season pennant odds today. Jimmy the Greek has the Cubs at 1 to 3, the Mets at 3 to 1, and the Cardinals, the pre-season favorites, at 20 to 1. Before the season opened, the Mets were 75 to 1.

4:40 p.m.

Ron Santo and Glenn Beckert of the Cubs are appearing on Kiner's Corner, the Mets' post-game show. A very sore loser Tuesday, Santo plays the gracious winner today.

"The Mets are no fluke," he says. Two days ago, he wouldn't have played their infield in Tacoma. "I'm not joshing," he adds. "They're there. They've got a fine pitching staff."

"I'm glad to see the Mets winning," says Beckert. "Of course, I'll be glad if they finish second."

4:45 p.m.

The Met clubhouse is quiet. The reporters gather about Gil Hodges' desk as he eats his post-game cup of yogurt.

"It was a good series," he says. "Anytime you take two out of three, it's a good series. I'm happy about it. Not satisfied, but happy."

Jack Lang, a baseball writer for the *Long Island Press,* walks in and takes a seat near Hodges' desk. He starts playing with a little statue of Charlie Brown that Hodges has placed in the middle of the desk. Lang takes the cap off the doll, puts it on his head, then puts it back sideways on the statue.

The room is totally silent.

"You don't have to answer this question if you don't want to," says Lang, reluctant to put Hodges on the spot, "but, did you notice any mistakes out on the field, besides the mechanical ones?"

"No," says Hodges.

The room falls totally silent again.

"Did the team let down today?" another reporter asks.

"It's not possible for anyone to be on Cloud Nine that long without that type of letdown," Hodges says. "We'll take seven more in a row and lose one anytime. The players are human, you know. This was just a bad game. No problem. We took two out of three. We're in good shape."

Someone asks Hodges what happened on the play in which Ron Santo was called safe in the second inning.

"Kranepool took his foot off the base, the umpire told me," says Hodges. "I could understand if he'd just blown the call. But to say *that,* he really blew it."

"If anyone should know about taking his foot off the base," says Lang, "it's you."

Hodges smiles. "I wish you'd told me that before I went out to argue the play," he says. "I could have used that line."

4:55 p.m.

The New York reporters crowd into the happy Cub clubhouse. After the Met victories, naturally, they had concentrated on the Met locker room.

"Here come the front-runners," cries Dick Selma, the ex-Met. "Look at them all come over here now."

5:00 p.m.

The Commissioner of Baseball, Bowie Kuhn, walks into the Cub clubhouse, accompanied by his sons—George, seventeen; Paul, thirteen; and Steve, eight.

"Hey, commissioner," yells Ernie Banks. "You brought us luck today."

"I can't guarantee the boys were rooting for you," says Kuhn, a bald, strapping lawyer.

Kuhn leads his sons into the manager's private dressing room. "Hi, commissioner," says Leo Durocher. "Nice to see you. I have a gripe to pick with you. What the hell do the umpires mean by, 'It's ump's judgment'? My ass, it's their lovable judgment. Well, sir, what do you say to that?"

"Well, Leo, without knowing the facts of the incident, I'd say it was the umpire's judgment," says Kuhn, who, in his first year as commissioner, has done such a good job Durocher calls him "sir."

"But commissioner, listen to this lovable story," says Leo. "We're in lovable Montreal and they have this big lovable hose they lay at the bottom of the outfield fence. Well, one day, the lovable ump says that a ground ball has gone under the lovable fence for a double. I run out and tell him he's out of his lovable mind. The hose is there, so how could the ball go under the fence? Well that lovable ass says it went under the fence in his lovable judgment. Well, sir, what can you do?"

Before the commissioner can answer, Durocher resumes.

"Well, commissioner, what do you think? The next day, that lovable umpire comes up to me and says I was right all along."

"Well, Leo," says Kuhn, affably, "as I said before, it must have been the umpire's judgment."

The oldest of Kuhn's sons has been listening to the debate. "Leo sure does have a nice way with words," he says.

5:00 p.m.

Gary Gentry, who took his shower more than an hour before the rest of the Mets, stands before his locker with a can of Rheingold in his hand. "The sponsor sent down two cases of beer for each guy on the team," says Gentry. "I guess I'll get bombed tonight."

"Again?" says a reporter, to himself.

5:05 p.m.

In the Chicago clubhouse, Leo Durocher is answering questions. Unlike Gil Hodges, Durocher does not always give a predictably polite answer.

"Were these the real Cubs today?" someone asks.

"No," says Leo Durocher. "These were the real Mets."

10:31 p.m.

The other New York team loses an exhibition game, 8–3, to their own farm team, the Syracuse Chiefs of the International League. The other New York team used to be the real Yankees.

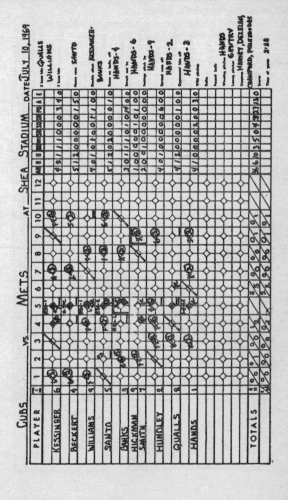

CUBS vs. METS at SHEA STADIUM DATE July 10, 1969

97

METS vs **CUBS** at SHEA STADIUM DATE JULY 10, 1969

PLAYER		1	2	3	4	5	6	7	8	9	10	11	12	AB	R	H	BB	RBI	SO	SB	PO	A	E
AGEE	8													2	1	1	1	0	0		2	0	0
BOSWELL	4													4	1	1	0	0	0		3	3	1
JONES	7													4	0	0	0	0	1		1	0	0
SHAMSKY	9													3	0	0	1	0	0		0	0	0
GARRETT	5													3	0	1	1	0	0		3	1	0
KRANEPOOL	3													4	0	0	0	1	1		11	1	0
GROTE	2													3	0	1	0	0	0		5	0	0
WEIS	6													3	0	0	0	0	0		5	6	1
KOONCE	1													1	0	0	0	0	1		0	1	0
GENTRY	1													1	0	0	0	0	0		1	0	0
GASPAR ph-pr														1	0	0	0	1	0		0	0	0
CARDWELL	1													0	0	0	0	0	0		0	0	0
TOTALS		1	0	0	1	0	0	0	0	0				29	3	4	2	0	6	2	7	6	2

Four

The Day
The Mets Collapsed

FRIDAY
JULY 11, 1969

NATIONAL LEAGUE STANDINGS
Eastern Division

	W	L	PCT.	G.B.
Chicago	53	33	.616	–
New York	47	35	.573	4
Pittsburgh	42	43	.494	10½
St. Louis	43	45	.489	11
Philadelphia	37	46	.446	14½
Montreal	26	59	.306	26½

Midway through the 1964 season, when he was only nineteen years old, Ed Kranepool seemed to be developing into the reliable first baseman the New York Mets desperately needed. Since they had Ron Hunt, an All-Star .300-hitter, at second base, the Mets lacked a reliable player at only seven positions.

On July 11, 1964, Kranepool was batting .296, and he had become such a fearsome hitter that, in the fourth inning of a game between New York and St. Louis, Ray Sadecki, the Cardinal pitcher, decided to brush the Met first baseman back from the plate. As Sadecki's delivery sped toward his head, Kranepool ducked. Mobility, however, was never his strong suit, and, in ducking, Kranepool managed to sprain his ankle. He had avoided the pitch, but he had to leave the game. Probably because his ankle ached, Kranepool's batting average slipped thirty-seven points before the 1964 season ended.

The Cardinals, of course, won the game, 11–4. The Mets, although they sank deeper into tenth place and lost Kranepool for a while, gained a personal season record: They committed six errors. One of them, an abortive attempt to stop a double-steal, was a wild throw by a Met pitcher named Tracy Stallard. Three years earlier, Stallard, then with the Boston Red Sox, had achieved baseball immortality when he served up Roger Maris's sixty-first home run. From that moment on, Stallard seemed destined to be a Met.

Only once in their history, in the first game of a doubleheader in 1968, have the Mets won a game on July 11. The victory lifted them only three games below .500, a height they never quite reached later than the opening week of their first seven seasons.

9:00 a.m.

The first edition of the *New York Post* comes off the press, revealing, in its sports section, the starting lineup for the 1969 National League All-Star team. For the first time, a Met outfielder has made the lineup. By beating out Roberto Clemente, Pete Rose, Curt Flood and Willie Mays, among others, Cleon Jones of the Mets joins Atlanta's Hank Aaron and Pittsburgh's Matty Alou in the starting outfield.

The selection of Jones—justified by his batting average of .347—seems appropriate symbolically, too, because he is one of the first pure products of the Met organization. He signed a Met contract when he was nineteen, only ninety days after the club played its first major-league game. He came up step-by-step through the Met farm system, from Auburn to Raleigh to

Buffalo, and, in 1966, he won a regular job on the parent club. He made the All-Rookie team in 1966, with a batting average of .276, and, after a disappointing sophomore season, became a solid .297 hitter in 1968, setting a Met record by stealing twenty-three bases.

Like Tommie Agee, his closest friend, his high-school team-mate in football, baseball, basketball and track, Jones won a college football scholarship, but gave up college to play professional baseball. His high-school baseball team, not surprisingly, lost only one game in three years. "Our pitching could've been a little better," says Jones.

Jones is the third Met ever to make the All-Star starting line-up. Ron Hunt opened at second base in 1964, and Jerry Grote was the catcher last year. Grote is batting only .225 this year and failed to receive even one vote in the All-Star balloting. In fact, aside from Jones, only one Met did receive a vote: Ken Boswell, who got precisely *a* vote at second base.

10:45 a.m.

In the lobby of the Waldorf Astoria, a few members of the Montreal Expos, who will play the Mets tonight, glance through the *New York Post* and examine the All-Star selections. None of them is particularly surprised to see that none of them was picked.

The Expos, in the first year of their existence, are not an awesome baseball team. Earlier in the season, they ran off twenty consecutive defeats, breaking the expansion-team record of seventeen, set in 1962 by, of course, the Mets.

Yet the original Expos, unlike the original Mets, are no joke, at least not at the plate. They have three solid .300 hitters—Mack Jones, a thirty-year-old outfielder who once hit thirty-one home runs for the Braves; Rusty Staub, a twenty-five-year-old outfielder who once batted .333 for the Astros; and Bob Bailey, a twenty-six-year-old first baseman who once collected a $175,000 bonus from the Pirates. They also have a twenty-nine-year-old rookie third baseman, Jose Alberto "Coco" Laboy, who, after ten seasons in the minor leagues, is batting .273 and hitting with power. As a team, the first-year Expos are batting two points higher than the eighth-year Mets.

There is a very good reason why the original Expos, unlike the original Mets, possess at least a sprinkling of proven, and still potent, talent. When the National League expanded to ten teams in 1962, admitting the Mets and the Astros, each of the eight existing teams was permitted to protect *all but fifteen* of the players in its organization. The new clubs could then begin building their squads from a pool of exactly 120 players, the aged, the infirm and the unpromising.

But when the National League expanded to twelve teams in 1969, admitting Montreal and San Diego, each of the ten existing teams was permitted to protect *only fifteen* players in its organization. The new clubs could then begin building their squads from a pool of roughly 1,500 players, some of them genuinely gifted.

Dipping into this huge pool, the Expos had little difficulty finding a few real hitters. The Expos did, however, experience great difficulty in finding a real pitcher. Not one starting pitcher on their staff has an earned run average respectable enough to mention. The best indication of the staff's collective skill is that Ed Kranepool is batting .444 against Montreal, and .208 against the rest of the National League.

11:00 a.m.

In the Met clubhouse, six of the team's pitchers line up in front of manager Gil Hodges. "Now listen to me, you guys," says Hodges, picking up a white piece of paper. "The commissioner has given a direct order. Anyone suspected of using grease on his hair for purposes of throwing a grease ball shall be immediately removed from the game. Everybody hear that?"

Tom Seaver, Jerry Koosman, Nolan Ryan, Don Cardwell, Cal Koonce and Gary Gentry nod. They are all in uniform. Hodges goes down the line, inspecting the hair of each pitcher. Finally, he reaches Gentry, who is fidgeting nervously, which is unusual for the confident rookie.

Hodges looks him over, then walks behind him. Gentry stands with the stone stare on his face. Hodges lifts Gentry's cap.

"Grease," says the manager solemnly, rubbing the pitcher's hair. "Gentry, you're the first pitcher ever sent to the showers without throwing a ball."

Gentry turns and walks glumly towards the showers. Hodges tosses him a bottle of greaseless Vitalis.

The video-taping stops. The first take of the commercial is over.

12 m.

Wayne Garrett, the rookie infielder, arrives at Shea Stadium. He goes directly to the clubhouse where he has an appointment

103

with Cal Koonce, the veteran pitcher, who has recently started selling mutual funds and insurance. Koonce is going to advise Garrett on how to invest his savings.

As Garrett walks into the clubhouse, Gil Hodges is standing in front of the Met pitching staff. "Listen, you guys," he is saying. "The commissioner has given a direct order . . ."

3:10 p.m.

"You're the first pitcher ever sent to the showers without throwing a ball," Gil Hodges is saying as the last take is finished. Gary Gentry walks back from the showers.

"I enjoyed doing it," says Gentry. "At least I didn't have to sing." He is referring to a singing commercial Tom Seaver has made for one of the Mets' sponsors, Royal Crown Cola. As a singer, Seaver is a magnificent pitcher.

"Originally, Cal Koonce was supposed to get sent to the showers," Gentry says. "But when they saw that he didn't have much hair, they used me."

4:45 p.m.

Jim McAndrew finishes an afternoon of playing with his two-year-old son, Jamie, and leaves his Hartsdale, N.Y., apartment for Shea Stadium. McAndrew is scheduled to start for the Mets tonight against the Expos.

"I would have liked to have pitched against Chicago, you know," he says, "in a big series like that and all, but this game is just as important. At least, *I* think so."

McAndrew, who was born in Lost Nation, Iowa, twenty-five years ago, played his first full season of organized baseball in 1966, after graduating from the University of Iowa with a degree in psychology. Last year he joined the Mets, who initiated him quickly and properly. In his first four starts, the Mets scored exactly no runs for him. Still, the tall, lean right-hander ended the year with a brave 4–7 record, on the strength of a fine earned run average of 2.28.

Without great speed, he depends for his effectiveness upon sliders, changes of pace and a surgeon's control. This year, his control has slipped, and so has his earned run average—to 5.32, the worst on the team. Still, like the rest of the Met pitchers, he thinks of the pennant and the World Series.

"Everybody likes to dream," says McAndrew, the psychology major.

5:55 p.m.

The Mets start dressing for pre-game drills. Most of the locker-room talk concerns a verbal attack on Gil Hodges by Ken "Hawk" Harrelson, the outspoken, flamboyantly mod-style outfielder of the Cleveland Indians. Harrelson played under Hodges in 1967 at Washington, and in the first installment of his autobiography, which is now running in *Sports Illustrated*, Harrelson calls Hodges "unfair, unreasonable, unfeeling, incapable of handling men, stubborn, holier-than-thou, and ice cold." Outside of that, he seems to like Hodges.

The Met players who agree with Harrelson—and there must be a few; no manager is universally loved—keep their feelings discreetly to themselves. Hodges' dressing room adjoins the clubhouse.

Several of the Mets are anxious to rebut Harrelson. "It's all just a publicity stunt to promote the book," says Jerry Koosman. "I tell you, he's lost one sale right here. I was shocked to read what he said. Gil Hodges is a gentleman's gentleman. I'm proud to play under him and know him. I'd like to be like him.

Then, his manager defended, Koosman goes on the attack. "I don't know Harrelson personally," he says, "but he probably never had any respect for anybody. He has his own problems and probably will the rest of his life."

Tom Seaver agrees. "Maybe Mr. Harrelson in his immaturity couldn't tell the difference between professional treatment and somebody picking on him," the articulate pitcher says.

"Gil handles players like men, not babies," says Ed Charles, who has played under six other major-league managers. "If someone wants to be petted, that's different. But if Gil hounds anyone, it's like a man. All I can say is he's done a wonderful job with me."

At the locker next to Charles's, Ron Swoboda refuses to take the whole thing seriously. "Those are the stock comments that could be made about most managers I can think of," he says. "I've heard that 'holier-than-thou' description of a dozen managers. Once you become manager, you get blamed for all the mistakes made on the ball field. It's a lousy job."

6:05 p.m.

In Gil Hodges' office, a reporter asks the manager about the Ken Harrelson article. "I've got no comment," says Hodges, who admits he likes his lousy job.

6:15 p.m.

Jerry Grote informs his Met teammates who haven't heard the afternoon scores that the Philadelphia Phillies rallied in the ninth inning to beat the Cubs in Chicago, 7–5. The defeat brings the New York Mets back to within one game of Chicago in the loss column. Chicago has lost thirty-four games, the Mets thirty-five.

"It's too early to start watching the scoreboard now," says Ed Kranepool. "It's a good way to louse yourself up. The only score we should be interested in is the Mets-Expos."

6:25 p.m.

Nick Torman, the clubhouse man, posts a sign over Al Weis's locker. With Bud Harrelson—no relation to Ken—away on army duty, Weis has been playing every day, including both games of doubleheaders. The sign reads: IRON MAN.

6:40 p.m.

Gil Hodges is sitting behind his desk, sorting through a huge pile of mail, discussing the success of his players. "Maybe," says Hodges, "they realize for the first time that it's just as easy to win as to lose—even in the major leagues."

Hodges' explanation works for players like Jerry Koosman, Tom Seaver, Cleon Jones and Tommie Agee, players who are capable of winning in the major leagues. But the rise of the whole club is not so simply explained. Hodges offers a more realistic answer. "When they split each of the leagues into two divisions," he says, "they made it possible for two teams to win in each league instead of one. Right now, we're in second place instead of fourth, where we'd be under the old set-up. Being in second creates excitement and feeds the belief in a team that it can win."

Perhaps the only team that hasn't profited from the new two division set-up is the Expos. Under the old one-division system, they would at least be ahead of the San Diego Padres;

right now, they are simply a distant last in the Eastern Division. "Are you glad the Montreal series falls between the two Cub series?" someone asks Hodges.

"No," says the manager. "If there's going to be a letdown, we'll see it tonight."

6:45 p.m.

Near the batting cage, Tom Seaver walks past a writer he met only briefly a year ago.

"Hi," Seaver says, calling the writer by name.

The writer is startled. "You're the first ballplayer who ever remembered my name," he says.

"New breed," says Seaver, a public-relations major at Southern Cal.

6:50 p.m.

In the dugout, coaches Yogi Berra and Rube Walker try to explain the sudden rise of the Mets.

"You used to be able to go out and sign up your own players," says Berra. "But now with the draft system, you have to wait your turn to pick. I don't guess there'll be any more dynasties that way." Yogi is still thinking about the other New York team.

Walker, looking toward Tom Seaver, is more to the point. "The reason is good arms," he says.

7:00 p.m.

Don Bosch, an outfielder on the Expos who once played with the Mets, wanders around the batting cage. Bosch came to the Mets in 1967, a year after his minor-league manager, Larry Shepard, who now manages the Pirates, announced: "In the field, Bosch can be favorably compared to none other than Willie Mays." When he arrived in the Mets' spring training camp, a blizzard of publicity suggested that Bosch was going to save the Mets. (The Mets used to have one or two such saviors every spring, more a measure of the team's desperation than the player's talent.)

Bosch was fine in the field, although his resemblance to Willie Mays escaped most people. At bat, however, Bosch couldn't hit the curve ball. And he had trouble with the fast ball, and the slider, and the change of pace. He couldn't hit his weight, and he wasn't very heavy, only 160 pounds. At the end of the 1967 season, Bosch and his .140 batting average were sent down to the minor leagues. The next season, he came back up and hit .170, and was sent down again.

Then, this past fall, the Expos purchased him from the Mets, and Montreal's bilingual yearbook proclaimed: *Bosch pourrait devenir une acquisition precieuse pour le club le Gene Mauch, s'il réalise seulement la moitié de ce que nombres d'experts du baseball ont prédit pour son avenir."* Or, in words familiar to Met fans: "Bosch could be a big plus in manager Gene Mauch's plans for the coming season . . . if he can just live up to half of what many knowledgeable baseball people have said about him." This season, Bosch is hitting .179, exactly what many knowledgeable baseball people have said about him.

As Cleon Jones finishes his turn in the batting cage, Bosch congratulates his former teammate on being elected to the National League All-Star team. "I voted for you," says Bosch, grinning. "Did you vote for me?"

Jones, kindly, says nothing.

7:02 p.m.

Ed Kranepool walks reluctantly toward the Met fan club room. A crowd of 300, mostly youngsters, awaits him. As he enters the room, he takes a microphone and starts answering questions:

"Why did you stop wearing glasses in the spring of 1968?"

"Who is your roommate?"

"Did you try to hit the ball to left field on Tuesday?"

Kranepool listens patiently and answers each question.

"I dropped the glasses because I had a bad start."

"My roommate is Tug McGraw. I roomed with Ron Swoboda for two years, but they broke us up this spring."

"I just wanted to hit the ball anywhere."

At the close of the session, the fans present Kranepool with two gifts for his son. The scowl that he wore on his way to the fan club room has disappeared.

7:15 p.m.

Gene Mauch, the Montreal manager, who fled the United States to escape Richie Allen, is on the field chatting with reporters. The carnival atmosphere of the Cub series has vanished. Television crews and newspaper columnists don't crowd around the batting cage when the Mets play the Expos, not even when the new Mets play the new Expos.

"Nice to see an opposing manager here," says Bill Quinn, who covers the Mets for the *Newark News*. "Leo didn't show his face out here."

"When you're in first place," Mauch answers, "you can do whatever you want."

7:20 p.m.

Until a month ago, Kevin Collins was one of the Mets' bright young prospects, even though the twenty-two-year-old infielder had never hit higher than .251 in the majors or minors. Then Collins went to the Expos in the deal that brought Donn Clendenon to New York. Now Kevin Collins is one of the Expos' bright young prospects. "Aren't the Mets going crazy?" he says, by the batting cage.

7:25 p.m.

The man who has been pitching batting practice for the Mets stands in the dugout, dripping wet. "I've been doing this for three years," says Tom Fitzgerald, who wears No. 61 on his uniform. "I'm a chiropractor in the Bronx and I fit my office hours around this. I'll be back in the office tonight. I throw about 125 pitches. I just try to get them over the plate. I used to be in the San Francisco chain, but I quit in 1959."

As the Mets' batting-practice pitcher, Fitzgerald gets paid $15 a night. "It's not the money," he says. "It's being part of something. This keeps me in the game."

7:55 p.m.

Jim McAndrew finishes his warm-up. He has thrown ninety-three pitches, but has not been putting the ball where he wants it.

7:57 p.m.

Francis X. Smith, the president of the New York City Council, presents Tom Seaver with a proclamation praising the pitcher "for the inspiration he has given New Yorkers in helping to make baseball come alive again in the city." Francis X. Smith is running for re-election.

8:01 p.m.

The crowd rises for the national anthem—the Canadian anthem, "O, Canada." Raised in Canada, Donald Grant, chairman of the board of the New York Mets and senior partner in the brokerage firm of Fahnestock & Co., stands and sings the anthem in French. He then sings "The Star-Spangled Banner," in English.

While Jim McAndrew takes his last warm-up throws on the mound, Grant talks about the new Mets. "This didn't happen all of a sudden," he says. "It's not a case of bums to heroes overnight. In 1962, when we started in business, George Weiss, who was general manager, said to me, "The other club, Houston, needs to win. We need to build. We've got to draft two things—nostalgia and young pitchers. Nostalgia to bring people into the ball park—Duke Snider, Gil Hodges, the old names of New York. After that, we need young pitchers."

Weiss's theory was better than his execution. The Mets got the nostalgia they wanted, but not the young pitchers—until seven years and several million dollars later.

8:06 p.m.

The first Montreal batter, Adolfo Phillips, a temperamental Panamanian center fielder who tied a major-league record by striking out eight times in a row in 1966, singles to deep shortstop. Jerry Grote calls for a pitch-out and catches Phillips stealing by such a wide margin that Adolfo heads back to first. Al Weis, the Iron Man, throws low. Ed Kranepool drops the ball. But the Expos do not score.

8:15 p.m.

The Mets announce in the press box that shortstop Bud Harrelson will return to the team tomorrow, a day earlier than expected.

8:26 p.m.

In the second inning, the Montreal pitcher, Mike Wegener, singles home a run to give himself a 1–0 lead. Wegener, drafted from the Philadelphia organization, won four games and lost twelve in the Pacific Coast League last year. He is 3–7 with the

110

Expos this year, the best won-lost record of any of their four most frequent starting pitchers.

8:40 p.m.

In the third inning, after the first two Expos hit singles, Danny Frisella starts warming up in the bullpen for the Mets. Frisella pitched for the Mets part of last year, but he has spent most of this season with the farm team at Tidewater, Virginia. He rejoined the Mets a week ago, and, two days later, pitched two innings in relief.

"When they took me out for a pinch-hitter," he says, "we were behind 6–1. And if you had told me as I was walking into the clubhouse that we were going to win that game, I would have said you were crazy. But we stayed in there and Donn Clendenon hit a three-run homer and we did win. That was the first time I got the feeling that this was a different ball club from the one I had played on last year. We didn't hang our heads and give up."

Frisella starts throwing harder as the Expos stretch their lead to 2–0. Frisella throws some fast balls, but his best pitch is the curve. "It's funny, being a relief pitcher," Frisella says. "If you're called, that means the team's in trouble. You hope the starter will do the job, and then you can sit. Yet you want to play, too. I suppose the ideal situation is to have a nine- or ten-run lead, and if the manager wants to rest his starter, then we can come in and mop up. But it hardly ever happens that way."

Jim McAndrew walks the bases loaded, and Frisella is called in from the bullpen.

8:48 p.m.

The Mets announce in the press box that shortstop Bud Harrelson will return tonight, two days earlier than expected.

8:51 p.m.

Danny Frisella delivers his final warm-ups on the mound, ready for his first official appearance at Shea Stadium this year. He almost didn't make it. He suffered through spring training with a miserably sore arm. "I called up Clyde McCullough, my manager last year at Jacksonville," Frisella recalls, "and told him my arm was killing me and I was thinking of quitting. He called me 'gutless.' So I stuck it out."

Frisella opened the season in Tidewater and, in his first start, ripped muscles in his rib cage. Completely immobilized, he used the time to lose fifteen pounds. "That picked me up," he says. Finally, in June, he pitched in relief for Tidewater, threw easily and won.

Now he walks the first Expo he faces, and Mike Wegener, the pitcher, steps in. Frisella throws him a high, inside fast ball. Wegener clubs the ball deep into the left-field corner. Three runs score. The Expos lead, 5–0. Wegener is now batting .313 for the season.

8:57 p.m.

The Mets announce in the press box that shortstop Bud Harrelson has returned to the club and is in uniform.

During Harrelson's absence, the Mets have won nine and lost seven, and his replacement, Al Weis, has done an excellent job. "Some of the guys at Camp Drum said, 'See, they can play well without you,' " says Harrelson. "Did they think I was hoping the Mets would lose without me?"

9:07 p.m.

Mack Jones hits Danny Frisella's curve ball over the wall in left-center field. The Expos lead, 6–0, after three and a half innings.

9:15 p.m.

The Mets score a run on three singles. Ed Kranepool steps in with runners on first and third, and one out. A man behind third base holds up a sign: SUPERDOOPERSTIFF. The sign is new, but the sentiment isn't. The critic in the stands is the same man who has taunted Kranepool with another sign: DAZZLE 'EM WITH YOUR SPEED, ED.

Karl Ehrhardt is the superdooperbannerfanatic of Shea Stadium. An employee of a display company, Ehrhardt has been making a display of himself for five years on Friday nights at the stadium. He has 120 self-made signs, but, for each game, he carries only half that many, indexed for instant use. His titles range from the straight-forward HOORAY, when the Mets go ahead, to the poetic BELIEVE IN MIRACLES, when the Mets fall behind. When the Mets take the field at the beginning of a game, Ehrhardt holds up AWE-INSPIRING.

"My greatest achievement this year," the former Dodger fan

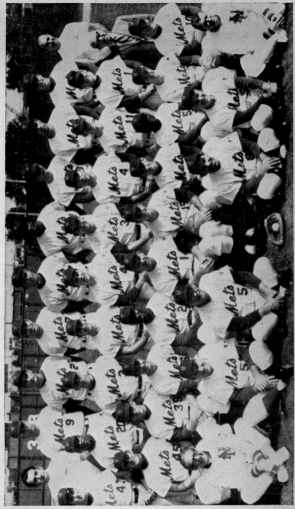

The New York Mets, 1969 World Champions. Bottom row, from left: Trainer Gus Mauch; coach Joe Pignatano; coach Rube Walker; coach Yogi Berra; coach Eddie Yost and Joe Deer, assistant trainer. Second row, seated, from left: Tug McGraw; Gary Gentry; Al Weis; Cleon Jones; manager Gil Hodges; Jerry Grote; Bud Harrelson; Ed Charles; Rod Gaspar and Duffy Dyer. Third Row, from left: Jim McAndrew; Tommie Agee; Cal Koonce; Ken Boswell; Tom Seaver; Jerry Koosman; Ron Swoboda; Wayne Garrett; Bobby Pfeil, traveling secretary Lou Niss. Top row, from left: equipment manager Nick Torman; J. C. Martin; Ron Taylor; Ed Kranepool; Don Cardwell; Donn Clendenon; Nolan Ryan; Art Shamsky; Jack DiLauro and Roy Neuer, clubhouse attendant.

New York Mets left fielder, Cleon Jones, climbs the left field wall to rob Chicago Cubs third baseman, Ron Santo, of a home run on July 10 at Shea Stadium.

Casey Stengel, the New York Mets first skipper, greets Mets owner, Mrs. Joan Payson, during the National League playoffs in Atlanta Stadium, October 4, 1969.

Mets center fielder, Tommie Agee,
spears a line drive by Baltimore's
Ellie Hendricks. Agee's catch saved
two runs. The Mets went on to win,
5-0, in the first World Series game
ever played in Shea Stadium, October 14, 1969.

Tommie Agee clutches Paul
Blair's fly ball for the third out
in the third World Series game
after Baltimore had loaded the
bases, October 14, 1969.

Mets right field-
er, Ron Swoboda,
makes a phenom-
enal diving catch
of Brooks Robin-
son's liner in
right center dur-
ing the fourth
game of the
World Series,
October 15, 1969.

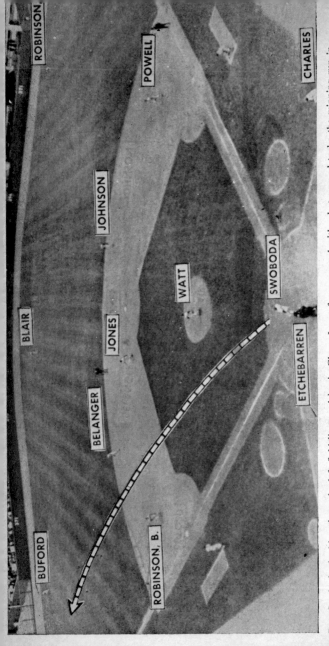

Ron Swoboda doubles along the left field line to drive in Cleon Jones from second with what proved to be the winning run in the final game of the 1969 World Series.

The moment of victory, October 17, 1969.

This was the scene at Shea Stadium seconds after the Mets won the World Series.

The banner says it all! October 16, 1969.

New York City Mayor, John Lindsay, pours champagne on Ron Swoboda (4) in the Mets dressing room following the World Series clincher, October 17, 1969.

Mets manager Gil Hodges is hugged by his daughter, Irene, and his wife, Joan, after the World Series victory. Smiling in the background is Gil Hodges, Jr.

Lower Broadway shows the effects of the spontaneous celebration which erupted as the New York Mets won the World Series.

All photos from Wide World

says, "came in the San Diego game a couple of weeks ago. Roberto Pena, the San Diego shortstop, became so interested in my signs that he stopped concentrating on the game. I was flashing signs about every ten seconds hoping someone would hit the ball to him, but they didn't."

9:18 p.m.

Ed Kranepool hits a fly ball to left-center field, not deep enough for a home run, but deep enough to bring one run in. The Expos still lead, 6–2.

Then Jerry Grote loops a single over shortstop, and Art Shamsky, the runner on first, stops at second. With two out, most runners would have reached third base, but Shamsky is not most runners, fortunately for most runners. His left foot points straight ahead, but his right foot seems to wander away from his body. "Gentlemen," Ken Boswell once said, introducing Shamsky to a busful of Mets, "I give you Ty Cobb." In a game earlier this year, Shamsky ran through coach Eddie Yost's stop sign at third and was thrown out at the plate. "It's all right to carry that piano on your back," his teammates kidded him, "but don't stop to play it."

On the next play, Al Weis hits a line drive at shortstop Bobby Wine's feet. Wine blocks the ball, but throws it past first baseman Bob Bailey. Shamsky, with Steinway on his back, heads for home. The ball bounces off the railing and straight back to Bailey. He throws home, and Shamsky is out by a step. The mild Met rally is over.

9:35 p.m.

"They come from places like Van Meter, Iowa, and Alvin, Texas, with arms that fire bullets," purrs the Rheingold television commercial at the end of the fourth inning. On the screen, a skinny pitcher, his jaws relentlessly working over a piece of chewing gum, moves to the mound. "And right away," the announcer goes on, "you know that this could be one of the great ones. But can he stand up to the test of time?"

The Rheingold ten-minute head looks stronger than the young pitcher. If he is one of the great ones, Danny Frisella belongs in the Hall of Fame.

9:37 p.m.

In the sixth inning, Mike Wegener, the Expo pitcher, drives home two runs with a single. His batting average goes up to

.333. With the score 8–2, Danny Frisella leaves the game. As he walks into the dugout to a cascade of boos and jeers, one beer-drinking fan serenades him, "Pack up all your cares and woes, flying low, to Tidewater."

9:41 p.m.

Another recent recruit from the Mets' farm system, a young lefthander named Jack DiLauro, replaces Danny Frisella. Di-Lauro pitched nine shutout innings against the Dodgers in his first major-league start and has gone downhill since. Still, he manages to retire the Expos in the fifth without further scoring.

As the Mets come to bat, Ralph Kiner, the TV announcer, switches the subject to the 100th anniversary of baseball. As part of the celebration, fans are balloting to choose the greatest team of all time. The television camera pans to the box seats. "And there is the wife of Babe Ruth, Mrs. Babe Ruth, who is a cinch to be the choice at that position," says Kiner.

It is not a good night for Met announcers, either.

9:43 p.m.

The other New York team breaks a six-game losing streak and climbs within nineteen and a half games of first place.

9:45 p.m.

In the sixth inning, the Expos open up an 11–2 lead, on a two-run home run by shortstop Bobby Wine, his first home run of the year, his fifth in four years. The Expos are hitting as if the Mets were pitching Tom Fitzgerald, the chiropractor, or the Rheingold kid, the one with the ten-minute arm.

9:50 p.m.

With no contest to watch, the fans are restless. A huge battle erupts in the left-field stands, attracting more than a dozen of the park's special policemen. No one seems to know what the fight is about. "Probably some guy said that the Mets couldn't catch up," someone suggests, "and they all started beating up on him."

9:56 p.m.

In the Met sixth, Art Shamsky hits a home run into the right-field bullpen. The crowd cheers as though the hit had tied the score. The score is 11–3.

114

10:02 p.m.

At least one fan is still watching the game, instead of the sporadic battles in the stands. The fan is wearing two buttons—"I've Got Pennant Fever" and "Let's Go, Mets." Her name is Ann Penner, but the baseball players know her as Baseball Annie. She works as a waitress at the dignified University Club on Fifth Avenue, but she spends many of her evenings at Shea Stadium, in seats set aside for her by Met pitcher Ron Taylor or coach Joe Pignatano.

Pignatano knows Baseball Annie from his Brooklyn Dodger days. She used to baby-sit for members of the Dodgers. "I was once interviewed for the '$64,000 Question,'" she says, "but they decided not to use me because I knew too many of the ballplayers and they might have been accused of giving me help."

Annie is the last of the old Brooklyn Dodger fans to come to Shea Stadium regularly. She cheers for the Mets, but, more than that, she is a baseball fan. She cheers for the Dodgers, too, and occasionally she'll go to Washington to watch the Senators, sometimes with Dean Rusk, the former Secretary of State, whom she met at the University Club. She exchanges Christmas cards with half the National League.

When Babe Ruth died, Baseball Annie stayed overnight outside the funeral home to be one of the first hundred people in line and receive a Babe Ruth Memorial button. It has a black border around a picture of Babe Ruth. Of all her mementoes, one is especially useful this evening—a Met crying towel.

10:19 p.m.

In the eighth inning, the Mets score one run and crawl to within seven runs of the Expos. The crowd, which couldn't care less, drenches Montreal's Coco Laboy and Bobby Wine with beer as they drift near the stands for a foul pop-up. A fresh fight breaks out in the stands behind home plate. Half a dozen Mets move to the edge of the dugout, watching five men swinging at each other.

"Like playing in Venezuela," says Tommie Agee.

"It's Friday night," says Ed Charles. "The fans have to have something to entertain them."

A fan near the scene of the brawl asks a special policeman

115

how the fight started. "When I hit one of them bastards myself, that's when I'll talk about it," explains the officer.

Lieutenant Bill Hall, in charge of the police detachment, looks over the chaotic scene. "We had 59,000 people and 10,000 more outside wanting to be inside the night Tom Seaver pitched and it was no problem," he says. "Tonight, a lousy 28,000. But there's no game to watch. What they had was that slush at fifty-five cents a cup."

10:24 p.m.

A white dog walks through a box seat entrance behind home plate, looks toward the scoreboard, sniffs the beer and walks out.

10:42 p.m.

Bob Pfeil flies out to left field to end the game. Montreal wins, 11–4, and the Mets lose a chance to gain a full game on the Chicago Cubs. Karl Ehrhardt raises his last sign: SAME OLD STORY.

10:51 p.m.

The Expos' clubhouse is cheerful, but not ecstatic. After all, the Expos are still twenty-five and a half games out of first place, twelve out of fifth place.

Mike Wegener is standing in front of his locker, savoring—more than his fourth victory of the season—his double, two singles and four runs batted in. "I never got that many hits before in one game," he says. "It's a first."

"What were you thinking about when you were at the plate?" someone asks.

"I just wanted to make contact," says Wegener, following the conventional script. "I just wanted to meet the ball."

Someone asks Wegener to compare the merits of the Cubs and the Mets. "Well," he says, "I never hit this well against the Cubs."

10:55 p.m.

Gil Hodges sits behind his desk eating a cup of raspberry yogurt. "To tell you the truth," the manager confesses, as half a dozen sportswriters gather around him, pencils poised, "I don't really like raspberry yogurt, but it's all they've got."

116

Hodges is smiling, not from any memories of the game, but because at least, as he faces his writers, he knows who is going to win this match. "McAndrew didn't pitch as well as he's capable of pitching," the manager says. "He pitched two good games and now he's pitched two bad ones."

What about the last three batters in the Montreal lineup collecting eight hits?

"They can beat you as well as anyone else," says Hodges. Then he pauses, reflecting. "They've got a bat in their hands, don't they?"

A reporter asks him whether he has anything to say about the Ken Harrelson article. He doesn't. Will he later?

"Probably," he says, still smiling. "But we could all be old then . . . or young."

"Is pitching your greatest concern now?"

"No," says Hodges. "Winning is."

One reporter gets up and heads toward the door. "I can't stand the quiet," he says.

"I can't stand the quiet, either," says Hodges, "but I can't leave."

11:00 p.m.

In the Montreal clubhouse, Mike Wegener is dressing quickly. He is leaving for two weeks of army reserve duty in Burlington, Vermont.

"Wegener hit so good," says Gene Mauch, "that he's riding home in a billionaire's jet. That's hitting."

Charles Bronfman, an official of the Expos, will be flying Wegener to Burlington in his private plane.

"He's the majority owner of the team," says Mauch. And then grinning broadly, he adds, "He also owns Seagrams."

11:14 p.m.

Tom Seaver walks by Bud Harrelson in the clubhouse. The Indians' Ken Harrelson is called the "Hawk." The Mets' 150-pound shortstop is called the "Mini-Hawk."

"Nice game," Seaver tells Bud Harrelson, who didn't play. "And nice comments about the manager."

11:15 p.m.

Art Shamsky walks away from the mirror, combing his hair. He runs into coach Eddie Yost. "Gee, I'm sorry about that

117

play," says Shamsky, remembering his sprint from third to home in the fourth inning.

"That's all right," says Yost. "They got a lucky break on the ball."

They didn't get a bad break on the runner, either.

11:30 p.m.

Nolan Ryan, a young pitcher from Alvin, Texas, with an arm that fires bullets, is scheduled to pitch tomorrow. He has watched the whole dreary game. Usually, the starting pitcher for the next day leaves in the sixth inning, but tomorrow's game is scheduled to begin at 4:05 P.M. The later starting time is a Met experiment designed to allow people to split a day between the beach and Shea Stadium.

"It's a good thing that pitcher won't be hitting tomorrow," says Ryan.

11:40 p.m.

Cleon Jones and Tommie Agee are the last to dress. Their lockers stand next to each other in a corner of the clubhouse. A reporter wanders over and starts talking to them about their high school days together.

"Our coach's name was Curtis Horton," says Agee. "I was a year ahead of Cleon in school."

"That's funny," says the reporter. "Cleon is five days older than you are."

"He's older," says Agee, "but I'm smarter."

11:55 p.m.

Wayne Garrett is riding into Manhattan on the E train. A young Met fan runs through the subway car and stops in front of a woman sitting directly opposite Garrett. "Do you have a pen?" the boy asks. "Ron Taylor's in the next car. I want to get his autograph."

The woman gives him the pen. The boy takes it, glances at Garrett for a moment and runs into the next car.

A moment later, the boy returns and gives the lady her pen back. He glances at the red-haired, freckled-faced Garrett again. The ballplayer looks barely older than the boy. The boy stares, then shakes his head and trots into the next car.

As he heads home to his Manhattan apartment, Danny Frisella is still replaying the game in his mind.

118

EXPOS vs **METS** at **SHEA STADIUM** DATE **JULY 11, 1969**

PLAYER		1	2	3	4	5	6	7	8	9	10	11	12	AB	R	H	BB	SO	E
PHILLIPS	5													4	0	1	1	0	0
SUTHERLAND	4													5	0	1	0	2	0
STAUB	9													5	1	1	0	0	0
M. JONES	7													4	2	0	1	0	1
BAILEY	3													5	2	1	0	0	0
LABOY	5													4	1	0	1	0	0
BRAND	2													3	3	1	1	0	0
WINE	6													4	2	1	2	0	1
RADATZ	1															0	0	0	
WEGENER	1													4	1	3	0	2	0
TOTALS														39	11	15	11	0	3

Time of game: 2:42

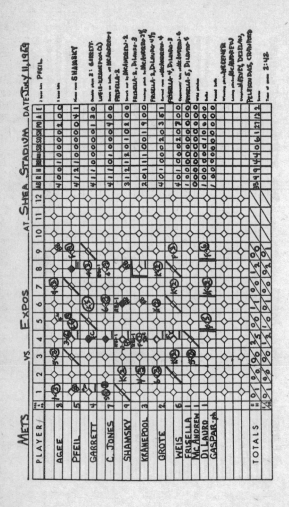

11:58 p.m.

"I just couldn't pitch," he says. "I was struggling. Either I'd miss with a pitch or I'd come straight down the middle with the ball. My fast ball was as straight as an arrow. My arm felt strong, it felt good . . . good and wild, like it wasn't part of my body."

Frisella realizes that, in another week, with Tug McGraw returning from military duty, he will probably go back to Tidewater. Still, the young Met pitcher isn't complaining. "This game's the greatest game in the world," he says. "I'm young and I'm single and I'm doing something every kid's dreamed about since he was six years old."

Five

The Day
of the Rain

SATURDAY
JULY 12, 1969

NATIONAL LEAGUE STANDINGS
Eastern Division

	W	L	PCT.	G.B.
Chicago	53	34	.609	—
New York	47	36	.566	4
St. Louis	44	45	.494	10
Pittsburgh	42	44	.488	10½
Philadelphia	38	46	.452	13½
Montreal	27	59	.314	25½

When Sandy Koufax was growing up in Brooklyn, the New York Mets did not exist. Later, when the New York Mets were growing up in the National League, they wished that Sandy Koufax did not exist.

Mostly because Koufax existed, on July 12, 1963, the Mets, who had lost twelve straight games, woke up confident that they could stretch their streak to thirteen. They knew, as well as anyone else, that the worst team in baseball was scheduled to face the game's best pitcher. The two had met exactly one year earlier, on the first July 12 in Met history, and Koufax had presided over the meeting, 3–0.

Naturally, the Mets never scored on July 12 until 1964. In 1963, Koufax shut them out, 6–0, and struck out thirteen men, including a pinch-hitter, Rod Kanehl, who was the most vesatile of all the Mets. Kanehl could, if pressed, play seven different positions, all badly.

Before Koufax finished his baseball career in 1966, the Mets did manage to pin two defeats on his record. In five seasons, they also pinned seventeen victories on his record. They didn't score a single run off him during a fifteen-month period, from early in the 1962 season until late in 1963, but they did limit him to only one no-hitter against them.

Since 1963, the Mets have never lost on July 12. They have won four straight games, including an exhibition against the other New York team, marking July 12—despite Sandy Koufax—as one of the glorious dates in Met history.

10:15 a.m.

Nolan Ryan, who is scheduled to pitch today against the Montreal Expos, wakes up after a perfect night's sleep. "If I'd been pitching during the Chicago series," he says, "I probably would've had trouble sleeping."

It has rained all through the night, and the skies outside Ryan's home are dark. "I hope we play," he says. "I don't want to wait another day."

11:15 a.m.

The rain keeps coming down, and Nolan Ryan, who still does not know whether or not he will play today, comes back from a trip to the corner delicatessen. He comes back without the salad dressing his wife wanted. She sends the scheduled starting pitcher back to the delicatessen.

12:45 p.m.

In the Met clubhouse, Gil Hodges, the manager, sits at his desk and, talking to a reporter, plays down his team's chances to win the National League pennant. "When you start talking pennant," says Hodges, "with a young ball club like this, in the second week of July, you're reaching for something I don't think is there. There's still too much baseball to be played."

But Hodges doesn't mind if his players want to think about first place. "It's better for them to think that way than not," he says. "It means they have the attitude that they can win every day. That's the only way to go to the ball park."

1:50 p.m.

Most of the Mets players are in their locker room, two hours and fifteen minutes before game time, and they hear the official announcement: The game has been postponed until September. The fans who might have split the day between the beach and the Mets now can enjoy neither. The rain is still falling, lightly.

"You going to the movies?" someone asks Rod Gaspar, the rookie outfielder.

"I don't go to the movies," says Gaspar. "It's bad for the eyes."

Rogers Hornsby used to say the same thing. Rogers Hornsby is in the Baseball Hall of Fame, with a lifetime batting average of .358.

Rod Gaspar is hitting .221.

2:00 p.m.

Sandy Koufax is at work for the National Broadcasting Company. With Jim Simpson, he is announcing the Game-of-the-Week, Pittsburgh vs. St. Louis. The Mets are very happy that Koufax is a broadcaster.

4:09 p.m.

The other New York team runs its winning streak to two games and moves to within nineteen games of first place.

4:55 p.m.

Three nuns come to visit Al Weis, the Met shortstop, and his wife, Barbara. One of the three nuns is his aunt, Sister Catherine Claire; all three are Met fans, who were supposed to go to the game at Shea Stadium. One of the nuns converted a few years ago—from the St. Louis Cardinals to the Mets.

5:02 p.m.

The game between the Cubs and the Philadelphia Phillies ends, with the Cubs winning, 7–4. The Mets lost half a game in their battle for first place. Rain-outs no longer are the Mets' finest days.

Six

The Day Cleon Jones Rested

SUNDAY
JULY 13, 1969

NATIONAL LEAGUE STANDINGS
Eastern Division

	W	L	PCT.	G.B.
Chicago	54	34	.614	–
New York	47	36	.566	4½
St. Louis	45	45	.500	10
Pittsburgh	42	45	.483	11½
Philadelphia	38	47	.447	14½
Montreal	27	59	.314	26

On July 13, 1963, a twenty-four-year-old pitcher named Robert Lane Miller, one of the original New York Mets, won as many games as he did during the entire 1962 season. Naturally, by July 13, 1963, he was no longer a Met.

Bob L. Miller—no relation to Bob G. Miller, another 1962 Met pitcher, except in ineffectiveness—was a premium Met, which means that, in the original expansion draft, he cost the club $125,000, or as much as the Mets paid for two other pitchers, Ray Daviault and Sherman Jones, combined. (The thought of Ray Daviault and Sherman, Jones combined is enough to frighten any student of pitching.)

In the Mets' first season, every bit as much as Marvelous Marv Throneberry symbolized the team's fielding skill, Bob L. Miller symbolized the team's pitching skill. By Met standards, he was absolute perfection—twelve consecutive defeats unmarred by victory—until the next-to-last days of the season. Then Miller committed his first, and last, victory of 1962.

At the end of the year, the Mets found Miller expendable, a terrible thing to say about anyone, and traded him to the Los Angeles Dodgers for two young major-leaguers, Larry Burright and Tim Harkness, who later, when they realized their full potential, became minor-leaguers.

On July 13, 1963, Bob L. Miller and the Dodgers beat the Mets, 11-2, allowing the New Yorkers to stretch a losing streak to fourteen straight games. During the game, the New York City Transit Authority announced that a big bass drum had been found in one of its subway cars. On the side of the drum was the slogan: "Let's Go, Mets."

No one claimed the drum.

11:00 a.m.

The New York Mets and the Montreal Expos are playing a doubleheader today, and between the games, the Garcia Company, which makes fishing tackle, will sponsor a fly-casting display. They would have had a better setting yesterday.

Outside the Met clubhouse, a man from Garcia gives Tom Seaver a spinning reel, and Seaver walks back inside to show off his gift.

"Hey look," says Seaver, a little puzzled, "it's a . . . a . . . a spinning reel."

"How in the hell would you know?" asks Rube Walker.

"I know about fishing," says Seaver.

"Ha!" says Walker.

Joe Pignatano rushes over. "Hey, lemme see," he says.

"What you got there?" asks Eddie Yost. Then, looking it over with a knowledgeable eye, he says, "That's nice. Real nice."

"It's a spinning reel," says Seaver.

"Yeah," says Pignatano.

"Piggy, what the hell do you know about fishing?" asks Walker.

But Pignatano doesn't answer. He, Yost and Yogi Berra are on their way out to talk the Garcia man out of some more free tackle. A few minutes later, they come back—empty-handed.

Walker laughs. "You wouldn't know what to do with 'em anyway," he says.

11:50 a.m.

The field is empty. The infield, protected until a few hours ago by the tarpaulin, is dry, but the outfield, after yesterday's rain, is a collection of small swamps. Neither team takes batting practice, but a few of the Mets wander out of the dugout and throw the ball around to get loose. As Jerry Koosman and Tom Seaver climb from the dugout, the autograph army lining the field boxes starts squealing for signatures.

Bud Harrelson peeks up from the dugout. "Jerry, Jerry, Tom, Tom," he pipes in good-natured imitation of the crowd. "When they walk out," he says, looking towards the Mets' two star pitchers, "I've got a chance to sneak out and get my exercise."

12:05 p.m.

Ed Kranepool sits in the Met dugout, looking as somber as a stockbroker in a falling market. Incidentally, Ed Kranepool is a stockbroker in a falling market. During the off-season, he works for the brokerage firm of Brand, Grumet and Seigel. Like most modern players, he looks upon baseball, too, as a business. "That rain-out yesterday cost the club a lot of money," Kranepool says. "They'd sold a lot of advance tickets. On the other hand, it's bad public relations ot make the fans sit in the rain."

Then, discarding his grey-flannel outlook, Kranepool looks at the rain-out from a ballplayer's viewpoint. "It hurt us," he says. "We've got a lot of doubleheaders coming up in September, and they really tire you out, mentally and physically."

132

But September is a long way off, and what hurt Kranepool most yesterday was a home run Willie Smith hit to beat Philadelphia for the Chicago Cubs. "After Smith hit that homer," says Kranepool, who watched the Cubs play on television, "I got sick."

12:20 p.m.

The Montreal Expos, in their tri-color beanies, which look like cutouts from a French flag, wander back and forth in their dugout, professionally aloof from the pennant race. They are the first team in major-league history to lose in translation. Because Montreal is a bilingual city, the team's guide book analyzes and profiles each Expo player in both French and English. The pitchers are *lanceurs,* aiming for *retraits au bâton,* or strikeouts. The shortstop to French-speaking fans is an *arrêt-court*—literally a "stop-short"—and the second baseman plays *deuxème but*—"second purpose" or, more appropriately, "second goal." All the infielders decorate the *intérieur,* and the outfielders are *voltigeurs,* which, translated, has them looping and soaring through the air like sparrows.

The *gérant* of the Expos, Gene Mauch, is *un ancien joueur d'intérieur,* a former infielder, who *a gagné ses épaulettes,* earned his managerial spurs, *à Philadelphie,* which means the hard way.

12:35 p.m.

Don Shaw, *un lanceur de relieve,* a "fireman" in baseball language, steps out of the Expo dugout. In 1967 and 1968, Shaw, pitching for the Mets, had the softest job in baseball. A left-hander with a corkscrew delivery, Shaw was usually asked to face one left-handed batter and shower. (This is stretching the truth only slightly; he actually pitched a total of sixty-three innings in forty-seven different games.)

After the 1968 season, the Mets decided they might survive without Shaw and put him in the expansion pool. The Expos made him their twentieth selection; so far, in 1969, they haven't worked him much harder than the Mets did.

"The Mets are for real," Shaw says. "With the pitching they have, they've got to be for real."

The Mets' sudden rise has divided rival National Leaguers into two groups—believers and doubters—and Shaw, as a believer, is a member of the minority. He wants to see the Mets win the pennant—that is, if his own club doesn't.

133

"I have to like the Mets," he says, "because I've got friends there. As a matter of fact, I roomed with Bud Harrelson at Camp Drum. I could see the Mets coming up long ago, because I played with Tom Seaver and Jerry Koosman in the minors, and they both had good stuff. I'm only sorry I'm not with them now. I could use a little extra money."

12:45 p.m.

George Vecsey, who is covering the doubleheader for the *New York Times*, enters the clubhouse, a book tucked under his arm. Several players notice the book right away, not because it's the first one they've ever seen, but because the front of the book shows the back of a shapely and naked young lady. The book is called *Naked Came the Stranger*, and the author, purportedly, is Penelope Ashe, who is, according to the book jacket, "a demure Long Island housewife."

Ron Swoboda looks at the book, checks out a few choice paragraphs and sees the description of the author. "Hey," he says. "What does that mean? My wife is a demure Long Island housewife, too. Does that mean she could write a book like this?"

12:50 p.m.

Jerry Koosman finishes warming up with catcher Jerry Grote. Koosman's overhand deliveries are sharp, but his side-arm pitches are giving him a little trouble.

He throws his eighty-eighth pitch and turns to his pitching coach, Rube Walker. "I feel fine," Koosman says, and puts on his warm-up jacket.

1:15 p.m.

After Jerry Koosman retires the Expos one-two-three, the Mets come to bat against Jerry Robertson, a fast-ball pitcher who never threw a fast ball in the major leagues before this season. Robertson spent four years in the minor leagues, primarily as a relief pitcher, and completed exactly one game. For Montreal, he is a starter, but not quite a finisher; in eleven starts, he has completed exactly one game.

Robertson retires the first three Mets in order.

1:30 p.m.

In the bottom of the second inning, Cleon Jones lines a base hit to left field, guarded, loosely, by Jose Herrera, a twenty-five-year-old Venezuelan. Herrera is hitting .370, higher than anyone else on either team, but he is not playing regularly, mostly because his fielding average isn't much higher than his batting average. In his first year in organized baseball, Herrera led the Western Carolina league in errors for a shortstop, booting the ball once every three games. Gene Mauch's decision to make a *voltigeur* of this *intérieur* is based largely on the hope that very few balls will be hit to left field.

As Jones's liner comes his way, Herrera tries to decide whether to lay back and take it on a bounce, or rush in and try to take it off his shoetops. First, he decides to lay back. Then he decides to rush in. The ball bounces at his feet and skids by. Jones reaches second with a double. Art Shamsky drives Jones home with a single, and the Mets lead, 1-0.

2:32 p.m.

By the end of the fifth inning, the score is tied, 2–2, and nothing startling has happened, except that Jerry Koosman has survived. He has already improved upon his season average of four innings per pitching appearance.

2:40 p.m.

As the Expos take the lead in the top of the sixth, a Met usherette accurately gauges the 3-2 score from her post at the bottom of the elevator behind home plate. Her name, she says, is Annette Ficucello, no relation to the former Walt Disney Mousketeer, Annette Funicello. "I always try to tell from crowd sounds what's happening," says Annette, who, when she is not tending an elevator, is attending the University of Miami. "At the Cub game Thursday, I counted five runs for the Cubs in the fifth inning, and that's just what they scored. I'm not usually that accurate."

Annette, a twenty-year-old Brooklyn girl, has been working for the Mets for three years and watching their games for seven. Until then, as a sub-teenager, her only baseball interest was rooting against the other New York team. "I just hated the Yankees," she says.

Once she started going to Met games, Annette got to know several of the players—an outfielder named Joe Christopher used to leave tickets for her—and, eventually, she applied for a job. She figured she was spending most of her time at the park, anyway. "My boy friends know that if they want to go out with me," she says, "they have to look at the Mets' schedule. If they're away, I'm home."

During the school year, Annette is a batgirl for the University of Miami baseball team. She got the job because she was the only girl in school with major-league experience.

2:49 p.m.

Someone hoists a banner behind home plate, announcing: WE LOVE KRANEPOOL. Ed Kranepool, unaccustomed to such affection, responds with a sacrifice fly that drives in the Mets' third run and ties the score.

3:20 p.m.

In the bottom of the eighth inning, Jerry Robertson, who is still threatening to pitch a complete game, walks the lead-off batter, Art Shamsky. Bud Harrelson then makes his first appearance since returning from army duty. Manager Gil Hodges sends Harrelson in to run for Shamsky, presumably because Harrelson got home from Camp Drum faster than Shamsky can get home from first.

Ed Kranepool steps up and twice tries to bunt Harrelson to second base. Twice, Kranepool fails; his bunts roll foul. Then he drives Robertson's two-two pitch into left-center field for a double. Harrelson, who doesn't carry a piano, races all the way home with the run that puts the Mets in front, 4-3. Suddenly, almost everyone in Shea Stadium loves Ed Kranepool.

Everyone except Jerry Robertson. Six outs short of the third complete game of his professional life, he is removed by the Montreal *gérant* and replaced by Dan McGinn, whose best pitch is his *courbe*.

3:27 p.m.

In the press box overlooking home plate, Harry Balberg steps up to a blackboard that hangs behind the row of New York sportswriters and, with a flourish, erases the name of Jerry Robertson and writes in Dan McGinn. Balberg, the official press-box attendant, posts the lineups, hands out the attendance figures, fetches hot dogs and beers and guards the press-box entrance "so that nobody can get in here without my knowing it."

Balberg is proud of the fact that he keeps injured Met players out of the press box—"Maybe the manager doesn't want the press to know who's hurt," he explains—but no one has figured out yet exactly why any Met, injured or healthy, would want to spend a game with the writers.

An enthusiastic Met fan—except, perhaps, on the days when he works the press box at Yankee Stadium—Balberg has made it part of his job to draw up a special scorecard for the president of the Mets, Joan Whitney Payson, whenever she attends a game. For Mrs. Payson, Balberg prints the names of the Mets in blue and the opposition in red.

Balberg, who started with the Mets as an usher and worked his way up, takes his post so seriously that he used to run Donald Grant out of the press box regularly—until he found out that Donald Grant was the chairman of the board of the New York Mets.

3:30 p.m.

Dan McGinn's *courbes* strike out three straight Mets, including Jerry Koosman. For Koosman, the strikeout is his fourth in a row, lifting his season total to twenty-five. With the season barely past the halfway mark, Koosman still has an outside chance to break his own major-league record, for pitchers, of sixty-two strikeouts in a season.

3:35 p.m.

The Mets look up at the scoreboard and see that Chicago has defeated Philadelphia, 6-0. They know they have to hold their 4-3 lead to stay within four and a half games of the Cubs. The Expos also see the scoreboard. They know that they have to rally to climb within ten and half games of the Phillies.

3:37 p.m.

In the ninth inning, Jerry Koosman retires the Expos, one-two-three, strengthening Philadelphia's grip on fifth place.

3:38 p.m.

The other New York team loses the first game of a double-header and falls twenty games out of first place.

3:54 p.m.

Between games of the doubleheader, three fishermen provided by the Garcia Company play "Cast-a-Ball" in Shea Stadium. The first fisherman tries to cast a ball—a foam rubber ball lofted with a casting rod—from home plate to first base; he misses. The second fisherman tries to cast a ball from home plate to second base; he misses. The third fisherman tries to cast a ball from home plate over the fence and out of the park; he succeeds. The crowd of more than 40,000 cheers. In other seasons, the Mets would have signed the man on the spot.

4:02 p.m.

As Nolan Ryan warms up with catcher J. C. Martin in the Met bullpen, the fans in deep right field gather to watch him. Ryan's arm always draws a crowd; sometimes, opposing players even wander over to watch him warm up. He throws with incredible power.

The Rheingold beer commercial—"They come from places like Van Meter, Iowa, and Alvin, Texas, with arms that fire bullets"—names no names, but, as far as anyone can remember, the only major-league pitcher to come from Van Meter, Iowa, was Bob Feller, the fastest pitcher of the 1940s. And the only major-league pitcher to come from Alvin, Texas—"The town's so small," says Jerry Koosman, "it doesn't even have a last name"—is Nolan Ryan, potentially the fastest pitcher of the 1970s.

Ryan is only twenty-two years old, and he still has a great deal to learn about pitching. His major problems are his control and his health. The first problem—when he loses control of his curve, he has no weapon to set up his fast ball, his best pitch—is common among young pitchers; his second problem is not. He has suffered through blisters, strained muscles and sore elbows, a one-man festival of aches and pains.

Since he became a professional baseball player at the age of eighteen, Ryan has enjoyed only one full season of good health, the 1966 season. He spent most of the year in a Class A league, stopped briefly in a Class AA league and then finished the year, even more briefly, with the Mets. In 202 minor-league innings, he averaged one and a half strikeouts an inning; in three major-league innings, he averaged two strikeouts an inning.

138

The following year, at Jacksonville in the International League, Ryan, rounding slowly into shape, struck out eighteen men in seven innings of relief pitching. For his first scheduled start, a crowd three times larger than normal showed up at the Jacksonville ball park. The crowd saw Ryan throw exactly one pitch, a warm-up pitch. He then announced that his elbow ached, and he didn't pitch another inning the rest of the year.

In 1968, at the Mets' spring training camp in St. Petersburg, Ryan seemed about as youthful and sturdy as most of the Florida town's residents. "He's got a great arm, but he can't pitch," said Johnny Murphy, the general manager of the Mets. "He's always got some kind of ache or pain." Ryan's teammates started calling him "The Myth." Gil Hodges gave him a chance to start against the St. Louis Cardinals in one of the Mets' final exhibition games, and suddenly, the legend came to life. Ryan struck out five of the first six Cardinal batters, pitched four scoreless innings and, at the age of twenty-one, made the Met team.

Ryan's bullets brought him a Met record of fourteen strike-outs in a game against the Cincinnati Reds, but they also brought him problems. The middle finger of his pitching hand tended to blister. Gus Mauch, the team trainer, eased the problem by dipping the troublesome finger in pickle brine—"I hate the stuff, I hate the way it smells," said Ryan—but still the young pitcher spent a month on the disabled list and lost his last four decisions.

Ryan, six-foot-two and 195 pounds, is both the hope and the frustration of Met fans. He has started four games this season and, although his statistics are impressive (3-1 record, 2.86 earned run average, forty-two strikeouts in forty-one innings), he has not yet completed a game. Now, in the bullpen, Ryan looks healthy, but his control does not. He is scattering pitches everywhere.

4:19 p.m.

In the first inning, Nolan Ryan walks the Montreal lead-off batter. One out later, he aims his fast ball—"Ryan's express," says broadcaster Bob Murphy—over the plate, and the Expo batter, Rusty Staub, aims the ball over the auxiliary scoreboard in left field. Montreal leads, 2-0.

One out later, Bob Bailey hits a ball into the stands, but these stands, fortunately for Ryan, are behind home plate. The foul ball barely misses a woman vendor at a souevnir stand.

She ducks and comes up shaking. "That one scared the heart out of me," she says. Bailey strikes out, ending the inning.

4:30 p.m.

Howie Reed, who throws knuckleballs, sliders, curves and change-ups, is the starting pitcher for Montreal. His style is the opposite of Nolan Ryan's, but his results are similar. He, too, hasn't finished a game he's started this season, but with a record of 4–2, he leads all Montreal starters in won-lost percentage.

Reed has a 2–0 lifetime record against the Mets, but he has not faced them yet this year. He started the season in Vancouver of the Pacific Coast League.

Tommie Agee, leading off, introduces Reed to the new Mets with a home run.

5:08 p.m.

After two and a half innings, Montreal leads 3–2, and in the Met dugout, Ron Swoboda paces back and forth, using up nervous energy. He doesn't expect to play; he is a right-handed hitter, Howie Reed is a right-handed pitcher and Gil Hodges, the Met manager, believes the twain should rarely meet. Swoboda figures that, at best, he'll get into the game as a pinch-hitter against a relief pitcher. "As much as I'd like to play every day," he says, "there are three outfielders having good years, so there's just no place for me."

Swoboda has been keeping himself in the game by shadow-boxing in the dugout, wrestling with teammate Rod Gaspar and questioning the wisdom of the umpires on moot decisions. Now, for a change of pace, Swoboda starts swinging on the rafters of the dugout.

Umpire Doug Harvey, positioned behind first base, spots Swoboda in action. "Hey, cuckoo," Harvey calls, "why don't you get out of the beams?"

5:15 p.m.

With two men out, Cleon Jones singles for the Mets. Art Shamsky comes up, and behind home plate, a tall, thin fan in a dark suit weaves to his feet, beer in hands, and starts cheering, "Let's go, Artie, let's go, Artieeeeeeee." The fan turns to the people around him. "No doubt about it," he says. "Shamsky's the best player on the team."

Shamsky swings and misses on a 3–1 pitch.

"Oh," moans his fan, "I've never been so disappointed in my life."

As Shamsky and his fan groan, Jones takes off for second base, trying to steal. The throw and the runner arrive at the same time, and as Jones slides in, umpire Frank Dezelan jerks his arm straight up, calling Jones out.

Jones has never been so disappointed in his life. Still on his knees, Jones tells Dezelan exactly how badly he feels. Jones indicates that he is disappointed not only by being called out, but also by Dezelan's personal habits. "I called him an angel," says Jones later.

Dezelan's arm flies up again, higher this time, ordering Jones out of the game. Jones expresses even greater disappointment, and Gil Hodges walks out on the field, to add his dismay. Hodges appeals, calmly, to Dezelan's sense of fair play, but the umpire decides not to rescind his verdict. As Jones and Hodges march back to the dugout, a sizable percentage of the spectators begin booing, hooting and hollering.

5:19 p.m.

Gil Hodges glances at his bench and signals to Ron Swoboda to take Cleon Jones's place. As Swoboda runs out to left field, the jeers, aimed at umpire Frank Dezelan, build to a roar. "At first," Swodoba says later, "I thought all that booing was for me, for having the nerve to go out there for Jones. I wanted to put my hands out and say, 'It wasn't my fault.'"

5:20 p.m.

Coco Laboy comes to bat for Montreal, and the howls of the Met fans intensify. White handkerchiefs wave throughout the stadium, pieces of fruit hail down on the field and, in every corner of the park, a chant erupts: "We want Cleon! We want Cleon! WE WANT CLEON!"

When Ed Kranepool drifts over to the box seats in back of first base, chasing Laboy's pop foul, a fan snatches the ball out of his grasp. Kranepool raises a fist, the crowd boos, angry with everyone, and the chant continues: "WE WANT CLEON!"

The uproar does not seem to upset anyone except the young Met pitcher, Nolan Ryan. He surrenders a double, then a single, and when the third batter bunts, Kranepool throws wildly to first base, allowing a run to score and advancing Expos to second and third.

Rube Walker, the Met pitching coach, goes to the mound to calm down Ryan. The handkerchiefs are still fluttering throughout the park, and the chant rolls on.

"WE WANT CLEON!"

"WE WANT CLEON!"

"WE WANT CLEON!"

Ryan walks the opposing pitcher, Howie Reed, and, with the skies darkening, the stadium lights go on, perhaps to show Ryan the way to the plate. But the next Montreal batter, Ty Cline, drives a single into right field, and the Expos lead, 6–2.

"WE WANT CLEON!"

"WE WANT CLEON!"

Instead, the Met fans get Jack DiLauro, a relief pitcher who comes in to replace Ryan. DiLauro retires the Expos without further scoring, and, finally, the crowd quiets down. Nine minutes of unbroken chanting have helped Montreal to a four-run lead.

5:30 p.m.

Annette Ficucello, the Met usherette, stops chanting along for Cleon Jones. Her work finished for the day, she is sitting in Gil Hodges' box to the right of the Met dugout. "Right now," she says, "I'm supposed to be at my uncle's birthday party. My mother asked me to go, but I said no. I've only left a game early once, when my brother graduated from high school, and I never stopped complaining the whole night."

5:34 p.m.

As the Mets come to bat in the fourth inning, Annette is all confidence. Art Shamsky singles, pleasing himself and his fan.

Ed Kranepool's pop fly drops in for a single, Al Weis beats out a bunt and the bases are loaded. Ed Charles comes up to pinch-hit for Jack DiLauro, and, on a full count, Charles singles up the middle.

The Mets have half of Annette's runs for her.

5:44 p.m.

Gene Mauch walks to the mound and signals that he is replacing Howie Reed, keeping Reed tied with Nolan Ryan and a few dozen other pitchers for the lead in fewest games completed in the National League in 1969.

142

Le Monstre—Dick Radatz, six-foot-six and 265 pounds—replaces Reed. A brilliant relief pitcher with the Boston Red Sox in the early 1960s, Radatz is now just a giant journeyman, recently dealt to Montreal by the Detroit Tigers.

Tommie Agee promptly slays the monster. Agee, who started the game with a home run, powers another over the right-center field wall, and the Mets lead, 7–6. Annette Ficucello, with her four-run prediction, was a pessimist.

5:56 p.m.

In the fifth inning, Doug Harvey, the umpire at first base, the one who had commented upon Ron Swoboda's antics, starts playing his own little game with the fans along the right-field line. Each time he turns to look at them, they boo him. He stares. They boo. He shakes his head. They boo. He puts his hands on his knees and looks toward the stands. They boo.

At the end of the inning, Shag Crawford, the chief of the umpiring crew, gathers his fellow decision-makers for a brief conference. Crawford points to center field, but nothing is out there except the American flag. Doug Harvey keeps staring at his shoes. After the meeting ends, Harvey is no longer playing games with the fans.

6:25 p.m.

The other New York team loses the second game of a doubleheader and falls twenty-one games out of first place.

6:32 p.m.

In the seventh inning—the score is now tied, 7–7—Bob Bailey of the Expos lifts a pop foul into the stands near the Met dugout. Baseball Annie, Ann Penner, camps under the ball, reaches for it and drops it. She is the last of the original Mets.

6:39 p.m.

The Mets look up at the scoreboard and see that, in the second game of a doubleheader, the Cubs have defeated Philadelphia, 6–4. The Mets know they have to rally to stay within four and a half games of Chicago. The Expos know that they cannot lose ground to Philadelphia today.

6:40 p.m.

In the bottom of the seventh inning, Tommie Agee walks and Wayne Garrett singles, with one out, the Mets have runners on first and third. The next slot in the lineup, normally, is occupied by Cleon Jones, who is batting an even .350. But now the next slot in the lineup, thanks to umpire Frank Dezelan, is occupied by Ron Swoboda, who is batting an even .222.

6:45 p.m.

Ron Swoboda comes to the plate, a symbol, probably more than anyone else, of the Mets in transition. Like the team itself, Swoboda has a tragi-comic past and the potential for a bright future. Unlike the team, however, Swoboda has a disheartening present.

Swoboda came to the Mets four years ago, only twenty years old, a chunky, broad-shouldered, raw outfielder who looked like a heavyweight fighter and sometimes fielded like one. In his first two months in the major leagues, Swoboda hit eleven home runs. Inevitably, sportswriters compared him and the strong man of the other New York team, Mickey Mantle. Of course, Mantle had more speed, but Swoboda had something Mantle would never have—a Chinese step-grandfather. In his rookie year, Swoboda finished with nineteen home runs—five more than Mantle had hit as a rookie—but still he was not quite Mantle. He was not put together along Mantle's graceful lines; he was built more like an armored car, in stature and mobility.

In the field, any resemblance between Swoboda and Mantle vanished. Once, in Cincinnati, Swoboda cost the Mets a game when he stumbled running up the outfield incline. Another time, in St. Louis, he misplayed a pop fly with the bases loaded and cost the Mets three runs and the game. "He's a little weak on balls in the air," suggested Casey Stengel, the analyst. "He leaps after them when they ain't there."

By now, mostly through hard work, Swoboda has developed into a competent outfielder, but he has failed to progress at the plate. Balls rarely threaten to hit him on the head any more, but he rarely threatens to hit them on the head, either. Opposing pitchers have taken to torturing him with breaking pitches, low and away, out of his power zone. He has cut down on his strikeouts this season—he led the team last year with

113—by shortening his swing. Unfortunately, he has also shortened the distances he strikes the ball. Once nicknamed Li'l Abner and Clark Kent for his power, Swoboda has become a singles hitter, and not a very good one.

6:46 p.m.

Ron Swoboda singles, a very timely one, a ground ball through the right side of the infield, chasing Tommie Agee home with the run that puts the Mets in front, 8–7. Cleon Jones, watching the game on television in the clubhouse, cheers for his buddy and for his replacement. He doesn't mind that no one is chanting: "WE WANT CLEON!"

6:58 p.m.

Leading off for the Expos in the eighth inning, facing Cal Koonce, the third pitcher for the Mets, shortstop Bobby Wine smashes the ball deep to left-center field. Tommie Agee, who already has two home runs, a walk and three runs scored, cuts across the outfield marshes, running like a fullback, turns on a last burst of speed, throws himself full out like a man smothering a fire with his body and grabs the ball just before it hits the grass.

7:00 p.m.

In the bottom of the eighth, Tommie Agee picks up a single, his third hit, and becomes the fourth man in Met history to score four runs in a game. The Mets lead, 9–7.

7:16 p.m.

More than six hours after Jerry Koosman's first pitch, Ron Taylor throws a third strike past Bob Bailey to end the game, with the score still 9–7. The Mets remain four and a half games behind the Chicago Cubs; six of the critical nine days have passed, and the Mets have won four of six games. The two victories today were not awesome, but they count just the same.

7:35 p.m.

Gil Hodges holds his post-game press conference. For the first time this week, he is not eating yogurt. He is eating a peach. But only his eating habits have changed. He still says nothing

145

revealing, nothing controversial, nothing he doesn't want to say.

Six reporters gather around Hodges in a semi-circle, waiting for nothing. Above the manager hangs a simple painting, which is either a seascape or a fresh photo of the Shea Stadium outfield. Behind the manager stands a plaque advertising an aftershave lotion called Brut. The manager's comments are dry, too, and softly spoken.

"I'm new here," says one reporter, keeping his voice respectfully low. "Why is Tommie Agee doing so much better than last year?"

Hodges has the answer: "Confidence." Then the manager adds, "What can I tell you? He's doing the things he should do, the things he didn't do last year."

"How do you feel about the Cub series?"

Hodges' face wrinkles at the question. "We have to go to Chicago next," he says, with a reply no more probing than the question. "That's what it says on the schedule, so that's where we're going."

"Is it difficult keeping the club up for a series with the Expos when it falls between two Cubs series?"

"We didn't let down," says Hodges. "We won a doubleheader."

As the reporters drift out, one asks, "Now, would you call the Mets a team of destiny?"

"No," says Hodges. "I wouldn't."

7:40 p.m.

In the Montreal locker room, someone asks Gene Mauch whether he thinks the Mets can win the pennant. Mauch knows about pennant races; in 1964, he took a Philadelphia team that didn't look like a great club—except when it played the 1964 Mets—and kept it up in first place until September. Then the Phillies lost ten straight games and the pennant. Mauch lost his job four seasons later, after a running battle with his star third baseman, Richie Allen, who loves everything about baseball except the hours and the Philadelphia fans. The dispute was resolved by the club management in favor of Allen.

"The Mets have the pitching that should keep them up there," says Mauch. "But the Cubs are too solid to catch. The big problem with the Mets is their bullpen."

7:44 p.m.

"Are the Mets for real?" a reporter asks Mack Jones, the Montreal outfielder.

"Nope," explains Jones.

"Why do you say that?"

" 'Cause they just ain't."

7:45 p.m.

The Met clubhouse is cheerful, but not jubilant. The players are learning to take doubleheader victories in stride, especially if they are over the Expos. Ron Swoboda sits quietly in front of his locker. Jerry Koosman straightens up the pitching charts. Donn Clendenon, who got to bat only once in the Montreal series and struck out, scowls.

Gary Gentry, the young pitcher, notices the two-toned wing-tipped shoes, with side buckle, being worn by another young pitcher, Jim McAndrew. "Check out those shoes," says Gentry.

"At least they're not cowboy boots," says McAndrew, the psychology major, to Gentry, the Arizonan.

"I'd rather wear boots than those things," says Gentry, hitting McAndrew in his ego and his id. "They look like the shoes my wife wears."

7:53 p.m.

A reporter walks up to Cleon Jones, the outcast. "What happened on that play?" the reporter asks.

"I thought I was in there," says Jones, matching obvious answer to obvious question.

Jones shakes his head. "I *know* I was in there. That's the third time this year that same umpire called me out on a base I'd stolen."

"Well," says the reporter, "it looked to me like the throw had you beat."

Jones smiles. "Then I'm sure glad you ain't no umpire," he says.

7:55 p.m.

Tommie Agee returns from the appearance he has earned on the post game TV show and talks about his past. "I can't describe how I felt all last year," he says. "Sometimes it was so

147

bad, I felt like I was numb. I didn't know what to do. I didn't know where to turn. A lot of the time I didn't even want to go out to the ball park. I didn't want to hit because I felt I was going to make an out."

8:02 p.m.

Across the locker room, Ron Swoboda talks about Tommie Agee's past. "He got the most vicious abuse from the Bleacher Bums in Chicago," Swoboda says, referring to the Cub fans who sit behind the left fielder in Wrigley Field. "They just might be the worst people in the world. Bleacher pigs is more like it. They yell foul stuff. They throw foul stuff. My wife and my mother are pretty sacred to me, but those people get some kind of perverted kick out of calling them names. Last year, during one whole game, they kept calling Tommie's wife a streetwalker. They're so damn ignorant. Tommie isn't even married."

8:45 p.m.

The Mets are on their way to see the Bleacher Bums. They board a bus that will take them to LaGuardia Airport for a chartered United Air Lines flight to Chicago. Hundreds of young fans crowd around the bus, thrusting scorecards through the windows for autographs. Ron Taylor, the pitcher, takes the cards, signs them and passes them along.

"Who wants to sign Tommie Agee?" someone on the bus asks, holding out a scorecard.

A member of the Channel 9 television crew grabs the card, scrawls "Tommie Agee" on it and hands it back. Taylor relays it to the youngster outside the bus. He studies the signature, then pushes the scorecard back to Taylor. "C'mon, c'mon," he shouts. "Now get me Cleon Jones."

9:15 p.m.

As the Mets file through the United Air Lines terminal, drawing a few stares and smiles and good wishes, the other New York team, returning from its long day in Washington, comes through the terminal, heading the opposite way. Billy Cowan, a former Met and now a Yankee—he's not exactly running in luck—spots some of his former teammates. "You guys are doing just great," says Cowan.

Ralph Houk, the Yankee manager, raises a fist in the air. "Go get 'em," says the ex-marine. "Give 'em hell."

10:25 p.m.

Aboard the chartered Caravelle, Ron Swoboda lifts his leg up on the seat in front of him and breaks the mechanism holding the food tray. The tray falls forward. "This happens to me all the time," he says.

Swoboda is not noted for grace. Once, at Shea Stadium, he caught a line drive and dropped his cap. He reached for his cap, picked it up, dropped it, leaned forward and kicked it five feet away. Even Swoboda laughed.

"We won a doubleheader today," he says, "and, it's weird, but it doesn't feel like anything special. We were just the better ball club, that's all, and so we won. We didn't play especially well. You know, we've never had the responsibility of winning before.

"It's getting scary. You see games you should have won and it kills you to lose them. You get butterflies. We have pride now, and it's a great thing. On a loser, you feel like a loser, no matter how you're doing personally. On this club, I feel like a winner."

11:35 p.m.

The seat belt and no-smoking signs flash on in the Caravelle. "We're beginning our descent into Chicago," the pilot announces. "The control tower asked us how you'd done today. When we told them you won two games, they wanted to put us on hold for twenty-four hours."

11:43 p.m.

As the plane glides toward the runway at Chicago's O'Hare Airport, a dozen Mets begin a pillow fight, laughing, giggling, shoving. Danny Frisella, the relief pitcher, watches and smiles. "Hell," he says, "the writers are the only guys who are nervous. This team couldn't be looser."

EXPOS vs METS AT SHEA STADIUM DATE July 13, 1969 (1st Game)

PLAYER	1	2	3	4	5	6	7	8	9	10	11	12	AB	R	H	RBI	SO	BB	PO	A	E	
PHILLIPS	8												5	0	2	0	0	0	1	0	0	
STAUB	9												4	0	1	0	2	0	0	2	0	
BAILEY	3												4	0	0	0	0	1	0	1	0	
LABOY	5												4	1	1	0	0	0	2	1	0	
HERRERA	7												4	0	2	0	0	0	2	0	0	
SUTHERLAND	4												3	0	1	0	0	0	1	0	0	
McGINN	1												3	0	0	0	0	0	0	0	0	
BATEMAN	2												3	0	0	0	0	0	0	0	0	
WINE	6												2	1	0	1	0	0	0	0	0	
BRAND	2												1	0	0	0	0	0	0	0	0	
ROBERTSON	1												1	0	0	0	0	0	3	0	0	
TOTALS													33	3	7	4	4	0			0	

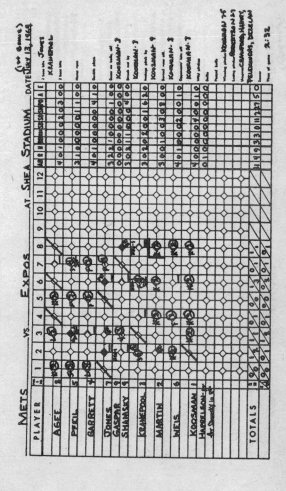

METS vs. EXPOS at SHEA STADIUM

(1st game)
DATE JULY 13, 1969

151

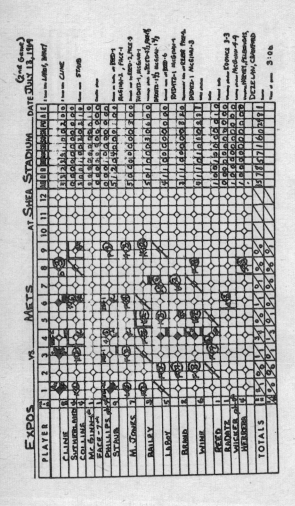

METS ___ vs. ___ EXPOS ___ at SHEA STADIUM ___ DATE JULY 13, 1969

(2nd Game)

PLAYER		1	2	3	4	5	6	7	8	9	10	11	12							
AGEE	8																			
PFEIL	5																			
GARRETT	4																			
SWOBODA	7																			
C. JONES	7																			
TAYLOR																				
SHAMSKY	9																			
CLENDENON	3																			
KRANEPOOL	3																			
GROTE	2																			
WEIS	6																			
DILAURO	1																			
RYAN	1																			
CARDWELL	1																			
KOOSMAN	1																			
GASPAR	9																			
TOTALS																				

3:06

Seven

The Day of the Bleacher Bums

MONDAY
JULY 14, 1969

NATIONAL LEAGUE STANDINGS
Eastern Division

	W	L	PCT.	G.B.
Chicago	56	34	.622	—
New York	49	36	.576	4½
St. Louis	46	46	.500	11
Pittsburgh	43	46	.483	12½
Philadelphia	38	49	.437	16½
Montreal	27	61	.307	28

If a single day could be eliminated from the calendar and struck from history, the New York Mets and Louis XVI would probably choose the same day—July 14. In the first seven years of their existence, the Mets played seven games on Bastille Day and, through such typical Met disasters as a missed squeeze bunt (1967), a misjudged fly ball (1964) and a Sandy Koufax (1965), lost all seven games.

On July 14, 1962, their first year, the Mets got an inkling of what was to come. Exactly 173 years after the storming of the French prison, the Los Angeles Dodgers stormed another monument, the Polo Grounds, with similarly devastating results.

While Walt Alston, the Dodger manager, sat and watched —he might as well have been knitting—his hitters beheaded the Met pitching staff. Maury Wills, who had hit no home runs in 1962 against the rest of the National League, hit his fourth against the Mets; Stan Williams, a pitcher by trade, hit a home run for fun; and Frank Howard, then a young giant, hit a ball 450 feet that took one bounce into the center-field bleachers for the longest ground-rule double in history.

Late in the game, John Roseboro of the Dodgers hit a high pop fly along the right-field line, and Marv Throneberry, playing first base, faded back to make the play. Marvelous Marv faded, he staggered, he twisted. "I've got it," he said. "I've got it." He didn't get it. The second baseman, Charlie Neal, slipped moving behind Marv and, lying flat on his back, perhaps from laughter, made the catch. In the next inning, Casey Stengel sent Gil Hodges in as a defensive replacement for Marv Throneberry.

Los Angeles won the game, of course, but Hodges' flawless fielding helped the Mets limit the Dodgers to seventeen runs.

9:00 a.m.

A bellboy at the Executive House Hotel in Chicago answers his phone. "No, he's not here," he says. "No. Call back after the game."

The bellboy hangs up. "The girls start calling the minute the team arrives," he says, "and they don't stop until the series is over."

Members of the Mets are strolling through the lobby, moving to and from breakfast, killing an hour and a half before the team bus leaves for Wrigley Field. The bellboy makes no effort to find the players who are being phoned.

"Why should I?" he says. "I've never seen such a stingy bunch of tippers in my life. I hate it when a ball club arrives. They want all kinds of service, but they don't want to pay for it. What the hell, they're not poor, you know. And we've got to make a living. It's not just the Mets. All the clubs are the same way."

The bellboy looks disgusted. "Ballplayers," he says, "you can have 'em."

9:30 a.m.

In Elmwood Park, a suburb south of Chicago, Larry Nestor leaves his home, a sheaf of papers under his arm. He is going to Wrigley Field to hand out copies of the fight song he has written for the New York Mets. His song is called "The Amazing Mets," with lyrics to match:

"The Amazing Mets, kin to the Jets,
Are out to win it all;
They know that they can do it,
'N' so they're sticking to it,
Determined to pursue it to the fall;

"The Amazing Mets, I'm taking bets,
Will come out number one;
Their pitching is bewitching,
And their lineup's strong;
A lotta fans are switching when they hear this song;

"Oh! Hail to the Mets, the Amazing Mets,
They're really on the ball;
They're gonna win it all."

9:45 a.m.

In the lobby of the Executive House, Ed Charles of the Mets, old enough to be called "Pops," still graceful enough to be called "The Glider," sits and talks about the pressure of a pennant race. It is a fresh experience for him, after eight seasons with the Kansas City Athletics and the Mets. "I've been in pennant fights in the minor leagues," he says, "but this is the first one in the big leagues. But the pressure's exactly the same, except maybe there's more reporters up here. I don't know how the young guys are going to handle it in September, but they seem pretty loose to me."

9:50 a.m.

Across the hotel lobby, Gus Mauch, the trainer for the Mets, sits and talks about the pressure of a pennant race. He trained the other New York team during eleven pennant-winning seasons. "This club may be a bit more relaxed than the Yankees used to be," Mauch says. "They're like kids who climb a fence. They don't worry much because they don't know how easy it is to fall and how much it hurts when you land."

10:25 a.m.

In Ray's Bleachers, a tavern outside Wrigley Field, Chicago's Bleacher Bums are gathering, building up their courage, singing their own fight song, written by I. C. Haag of Northbrook, Illinois. Haag explains that his initials stand for Incredibly Creative. His lyrics dispute him:

> "Hey, hey!
> Holy Mackerel! !
> No doubt about it! ! !
> The Cubs are on their way—Hey! Hey!

> "The Cubs are gonna HIT today,
> They're gonna PITCH today,
> They're gonna FIELD today;
> Come what may—the Cubs are gonna WIN today!"

The Bums were spawned several years ago by a woman named Ma Barker and her husband. "It was really my husband who started it," says Ma Barker. "He had a sign with a target painted on it, and a hole in the middle, and it said: 'Hit a Bleacher Bum.' When Ron Santo came up, we'd take turns putting our heads through the middle, hoping that Santo would hit us."

Now there are some seventy-five hard-core Bums in the bleachers, with their own special uniform—a yellow construction hat, designed to keep out the sun, garbage, flying beer cans and bottles—and their own public relations man, a Bum named Don.

The Bums are worried about their image—they've been blamed lately for everything from spitting on opponents to starting the Chicago fire—and, so, today, their P.R. man shows reporters around Ray's Bleachers, stands with them at the bleacher ticket window and guides them inside the park. Under the leadership of their president, Ron Grousl, the Bums, who don't want to get a bad name, have instituted "Operation Finger," a program requiring each Bum to report to the security police anyone he sees throwing objects on the playing field. The most memorable object to come flying out of the left-field bleachers in recent weeks was a pair of crutches.

10:30 a.m.

The World Series fever that infected New York last week, three months out of season, is now running through Chicago. Already, 200 ushers are circling the stadium to handle the swelling crowd. The Chicago police force has assigned twenty-eight patrolmen and three sergeants to help out the regular security police at Wrigley Field. It is almost as exciting as a Democratic National Convention.

One middle-aged man shows up at the ticket window, carrying a six-pack of beer, uncamouflaged, undisguised, out in the open. Lieutenant Ed Mowen, who has been policing Wrigley Field for more than a quarter of a century, explains to the man that he can't bring beer into the ball park. "Don't you know the regulations?" says Mowen.

"No," says the beer-carrier. "This is the first time I've been to Wrigley Field in twenty-five years."

11:05 a.m.

As the Mets' team bus cruises past stretches of sandy beach along Lake Michigan, Dick Young of the *New York Daily News*, who has been covering baseball in New York with wit and perception since the end of World War II, talks about the Met chances. Young is a realist, who can be funny and barbed at the same time. "The tree that grows in Brooklyn is an apple tree," he once wrote, when the Dodgers were slipping in the pennant race and the book *A Tree Grows in Brooklyn* was climbing the best-seller lists, "and all the apples are in the throats of the Dodgers."

Young is more tolerant of the young Mets. "I picked the Cardinals to win this division in the spring," he says, "and I still think they will. They're the only class team in the division, and I believe that class will tell over 162 games.

"The Mets didn't expect to win the pennant this year, and I don't think they'll be too disappointed if they don't. This team isn't particularly hungry for money. It's hungry for achievement. Still, if the Cardinals don't make their move, the Mets have a chance to take it all."

12:05 p.m.

In Henry's Hamburgers, a milk-shake version of Ray's Bleachers and the hangout for the under-twenty-one Bleacher Bums, a Chicago high-school senior named Bill Strunck orders a Coke. Four years ago, Strunck, a Cub fan since childhood, grew disillusioned and, conditioned to disaster, decided to switch to the Mets. In 1966, the Cubs rewarded his lack of faith by finishing behind the Mets.

Strunck is wearing a Mets cap. Across the aisle, a couple of yellow-helmeted Bleacher Bums stare at him coldly. One of them rises and shouts a standard Bum cheer: "Two bits, four bits, six bits, a comet, all for the Mets stand up and vomit!"

Then the cheerleader, a deeply-tanned and freckled twenty-year-old, walks over to Strunck's table and, with a Marlon Brando swagger, removes the Mets cap. "We found a guy wearing one of these in the bleachers a couple of months ago," says the Bum, "and we used lighter fluid on it. Now, don't let us see this thing around again or you'll lose it."

Strunck slips the Mets cap in his back pocket and finishes his Coke.

12:20 p.m.

Tom Seaver, who is pitching today, his first start since his near-perfect game, sits alone in the Met clubhouse. Jim Brosnan, the former major-league pitcher, now an author working on a book about Ron Santo of the Cubs, comes into the clubhouse and spots Seaver. "Don't you take batting practice?" says Brosnan.

"The way I hit," says Seaver, "I better."

Brosnan nods; he understands.

12:22 p.m.

Tom Seaver emerges from the Met dugout and heads toward the batting cage. With his blond hair and boyish good looks, he might have stepped out of an *Esquire* shirt ad or off a Peace Corps poster. Immediately, he is engulfed by reporters, cameramen and announcers. Seaver, his mind on the game, says a few words to everyone, then steps into the cage for his swings.

161

Seaver takes a few cuts and returns to the dugout. "Hit any out?" someone asks, knowing the answer.

"No," says Seaver. "But I got a couple of singles."

12:30 p.m.

Ernie Banks of the Cubs is interviewing Cleon Jones of the Mets. Banks, besides playing first base and hitting homes runs, conducts his own pre-game radio show and his own newspaper column. Jones is not about to feed Banks anything controversial for his show or his column.

"The Cubs are the toughest team for me," says Jones, politely, overlooking the fact that he has driven in ten runs in eleven games against Chicago this year.

"You're having a great year," says Banks, politely. "You're one of the best hitters in the league."

"It's all concentration," says Jones. "I'm concentrating more this year."

12:40 p.m.

"You nervous?" a reporter asks Randy Hundley, the Chicago catcher.

"Nah," says Hundley. "We're gonna take 'em."

12:50 p.m.

"Big series for you, isn't it?" a reporter asks Donn Clendenon, the Met first baseman.

"Nah," says Clendenon. "We're gonna take 'em."

1:00 p.m.

A Chicago reporter walks up to Al Weis, one of three former White Sox on the Mets, and asks the skinny infielder about the difference between playing for the Mets, battling Chicago for the pennant, and playing for the White Sox, battling the Yankees for the pennant.

"There's more enthusiasm on this club," says Weis. "We've got a lot of kids. In some of the games we've won, the players have run onto the field and carried guys off. You only see that kind of thing in the World Series."

1:05 p.m.

The World Series atmosphere surrounding the Cub-Met games is a pleasant one for Lindsey Nelson, who, with Bob Murphy and Ralph Kiner, has been broadcasting the Met games since the team began. Among them, the three men have reported more disasters than anyone since the Johnstown telephone operators.

Nelson, eating his pre-game meal in the press room, explains that the new Mets have made his job easier. "Anyone can broadcast a winner," he says. "But what do you do when you're behind, 11-0, in the third inning and you've got six more innings to go? What do you say after you say you're sorry?"

1:10 p.m.

As Tom Seaver warms up in the bullpen, troubled by a slight stiffness in his right shoulder, Danny Frisella, the relief pitcher recently recalled from Tidewater, reminisces about the first time he and Seaver were teammates. In the summer of 1965, they both pitched in Fairbanks, Alaska, for the Alaska Gold-panners.

"The team was put together by a man named Red Boucher," says Frisella. "He's mayor of Fairbanks now. He got all the best young ballplayers up there—Andy Messersmith, who pitches for the Angels now; Mike Paul, who's with Cleveland; Graig Nettles of Minnesota. Steve Sogge, the Southern Cal quarterback, played up there, and so did Rick Monday of Oakland. Monday was there the year I was and he couldn't even make our team. I think thirteen guys were signed off that team. It was semi-pro ball, and we played eight games a week. We didn't get paid. Not for playing ball. But I earned $650 a month for pulling a lever on a dump truck. And I didn't have to pull the lever too often."

1:25 p.m.

Pat Pieper, the field announcer for the Chicago Cubs since 1906, reads off the starting lineups. He has lived through Tinker-to-Evers-to-Chance. He has lived through Hack Wilson and Hank Sauer. He saw the Cubs win the world championship twice in his first three years. He has been waiting sixty years to see them do it once more. He is probably the calmest man in the ball park.

"I never get World Series fever until September," says Pieper, who wears a windbreaker and a green baseball cap of no discernible allegiance. "I've seen too many surprises in this game. In the 1918 World Series between the Cubs and the Boston Red Sox, I saw Babe Ruth lifted for a pinch-hitter."

1:30 p.m.

As "The Star-Spangled Banner" is played, reporters, columnists and magazine writers crowd into the Chicago press box. The place hasn't been so jammed in almost a quarter of a century, not since 1945, the last time the Cubs won the National League pennant, the year Tom Seaver celebrated his first birthday.

Two Chicago writers—one working for a wire service, the other a newspaper columnist—start arguing over the last free chair. The columnist takes possession. "I sit here every day," argues the wire-service man. "See—that's my telephone."

"I don't give a damn whose telephone it is," says the columnist. "I'm not moving unless you can find me a better seat."

The press box attendant diplomatically squeezes in another chair.

1:32 p.m.

As soon as the national anthem ends and the crowd offers its ritual applause, another song floats over the public address system: "Hey, Hey, Holy Mackerel!" The Bleacher Bums cheer happily, and I. C. Haag feels the same pride Irving Berlin must feel every time he encounters carolers singing "White Christmas."

1:34 p.m.

Banners and signs and posters are on display all over Wrigley Field. The Ron Santo fans call for PIZZA POWER, a reference to Santo's Italian heritage, and the Randy Hundley fans honor REBEL RANDY, a tribute to the catcher's Virginia heritage. HEY, HEY, POW WOW CUBS boosts the whole team, and, in the bleachers, a group of fans unfurl a twenty-six-foot long banner showing that their allegiance has shifted: MILWAUKEE SAYS GO GET 'EM BRAVES CUBS.

In the lower left-field stands, a group of ten teenagers, male and female, run through the aisles, toting a cardboard sign inscribed with colored pencil: LONG BEACH AND WOODMERE ARE WITH YOU, METS!

The youngsters, chanting, "Yay, Mets," are Long Islanders studying at Northwestern University's summer institute for high-school students planning to major in education. Their demonstration for the Mets takes the Cub fans around them by surprise. The Cub fans are so surprised that they do not pelt the teenagers with crushed paper cups and peanut shells —not until they reach their seats.

1:35 p.m.

Bill Hands, who snapped the Cub losing streak in New York last week and scored his fifth straight victory over the Mets, is the starting pitcher for Chicago.

In the first inning Hands retires the Mets, one-two-three.

1:40 p.m.

In the first inning, Tom Seaver retires the Cubs, one-two-three, striking out two of them.

2:20 p.m.

Five days too late for perfection, Tom Seaver gets Jim Qualls to ground out to first base.

2:25 p.m.

The Mets and the Cubs move into the fourth inning, with the score tied, 0–0. Bill Hands has allowed the Mets only a pair of singles, and Tom Seaver has allowed the Cubs nothing. The Met star has set down the first nine Cubs in order, just as he did last Wednesday night.

On the record, Seaver looks every bit as effective as he did in his last appearance, yet there are perceptible differences. He is not getting his breaking pitches exactly where he wants them, and instead of throwing them for strikes, he is using them to set up his fast ball. He is throwing far more pitches than he did last week; he is falling behind batters far more often. Even if the casual fan can't tell the difference, Seaver can. He isn't happy with himself. "Sometimes everything is perfect right from the first pitch," he says later. "Sometimes you don't get it until the third inning. Sometimes never. I went out there today and knew I didn't have it."

Still, Seaver without it is better than most pitchers with it.

2:35 p.m.

As the Cubs come to bat in the bottom of the fourth, their fans start chanting, "Go, go, go." One of the cheerleaders, as usual at Wrigley Field, is an usher named Malcolm Reeser, who is dancing on a catwalk leading from the grandstand to the press box and television camera booths. He is clapping his hands, dancing a jig and whirling his arms, urging the Cubs on. A tall, thin man, Reeser is seventy years old.

Don Kessinger, who will be twenty-seven in three days, leads off with a ground ball to second base. Ken Boswell of the Mets grabs the ball, drops it, picks it up and throws to first in time to get Kessinger. "Boswell," says a New York sportswriter in the press box, "is a prime candidate for a hand transplant."

Glenn Beckert then beats out an infield hit up the middle, and Billy Williams drives a single into right field. The Cubs have men on first and third with one out, and, now, the pressure is on Tom Seaver. The Cubs have their top run-producers, Ron Santo and Ernie Banks, coming up.

Seaver responds perfectly. He strikes out Santo and Banks.

3:01 p.m.

The game is still scoreless going into the bottom of the sixth inning. The Mets have three singles, the Cubs two. With one out, Don Kessinger beats out a bunt, to even the singles, and in the small park, the roar of some 40,000 spectators sounds like a single squeal amplified 40,000 times.

Tom Seaver works carefully to Glenn Beckert, hoping that he can strike him out (unlikely; Beckert has struck out only nine times in 258 times at bat) or get him to pop up. But, somehow, on a high inside fast ball, Beckert grounds the ball weakly toward second base. Ken Boswell charges the ball and, with his own hands, scoops it up and throws Beckert out at first. But Kessinger has advanced to second, into scoring position, exactly what Seaver had hoped to avoid. "I don't know how Beckert hit that ball to second base," Seaver says later. "It was a perfect pitch. I'd throw it again."

Again, the pressure is on Seaver, facing Billy Williams.

This time, Williams responds perfectly. The left-handed hitter lines a fast ball over shortstop and into left-center field. Kessinger scores the first Cub run off Seaver in eighteen innings—a streak spanning three different games—and Chicago leads, 1–0.

3:11 p.m.

Only a handful of fans stand and stretch as the Mets come to bat in the seventh inning. And, of those few, only one is not hooted or pelted or insulted. She stands quietly in the left-field grandstand. Her hand, which holds a transistor radio, is raised to her ear inside the hood of her nun's habit.

3:14 p.m.

With one out in the seventh inning, J. C. Martin, the Met catcher, walks to the plate. All three ex-White Sox are in New York's starting lineup today. Martin hits the first pitch deep to right field. It appears for a moment as though the game is tied, but the wind is blowing in at Wrigley Field. The ball crashes into the wall just a foot below the bleacher railing. Jim Qualls, racing over from center field, retrieves the ball quickly and Martin, running less quickly, stops at second. He gets no farther. The other two ex-White Sox, Al Weis and Tommie Agee, make the second and third outs.

3:28 p.m.

Ernie Banks, who has singled to start the seventh inning for Chicago, stands on first base. "Do you suppose Seaver is second-guessing himself on that pitch to Williams?" Banks asks Ed Kranepool.

"I don't know," says Kranepool. "He's pitching. Go ask him."

Banks stays on first base. "I think if he had asked Tom," says Kranepool later, "he might have wound up on his ass his next time up."

3:35 p.m.

The official attendance at Wrigley Field is 37,473, but the old park, which looks like a pile of bleachers set into a steel frame, seems to be sagging under the weight of a standing-room crowd closer to 45,000.

3:41 p.m.

Ken Boswell leads off for the Mets in the eighth inning. He swings late on a fast ball. The ball hits third base—a fair ball —then twists into foul territory down the left-field line. Boswell rounds first and sees Billy Williams, in left field, dashing toward the ball. "Whoa, whoa, whoa," yells Yogi Berra, coaching a first base.

Boswell ignores Berra's advice. He feels certain he can reach second before Williams can retrieve the ball.

But Boswell has failed to notice Ron Santo, sprinting toward the ball from third base. Santo gets to the ball. "Throw it to second," he tells himself, without looking up. "He got a slow start." Santo's peg to second base beats Boswell by two steps. Boswell is out.

"It was the wrong play," Gil Hodges says later. "You have to have a much better shot at it before you try for two bases. You're the lead-off man and the next batter is the league's second leading hitter. It was a mistake, but we all make them."

3:43 p.m.

Behind home plate, two men in dark suits groan when Ken Boswell is called out. Both men are in their early twenties, both are Met fans and both are A.W.O.L. from their jobs in New York. Weeks ago, they had ordered tickets for this game, and this morning they called in sick to their employer, the New York City Board of Education, then flew to Chicago.

They missed the first inning of the game because of a mathematical error. Before they left New York, they set their watches back an hour, from ten o'clock to nine. Once they arrived in Chicago, they forgot they had set their watches back and continued to subtract an hour. They reached Wrigley Field at 1:45 P.M., thinking it was only 12:45.

Boswell's timing was no better, and now, as the two New Yorkers show their disappointment, a man sitting nearby, with his wife and his brother, turns around. "Hey, you're Met fans, too," he says. "So are we."

A gray-haired man sitting next to the two Board of Education employees overhears the exchange. "I came to see 'em win, too," he says. All six Met fans have hidden their feelings for seven innings, trying not to disturb the natives, but now they all begin cheering loudly, ignoring the abuse hurled at them.

3:46 p.m.

With Art Shamsky at bat in the eighth inning, manager Gil Hodges tells Rod Gaspar that, if Shamsky gets a hit, Gaspar will go in to run for him. Shamsky doesn't get a hit; he makes the final out of the inning. But Gaspar assumes that the manager wants him to go into right field, anyway, as a defensive replacement. The rookie grabs his glove and heads toward the outfield.

"Who is that?" says Pat Pieper, the veteran Chicago announcer, as he spots Gaspar trotting onto the field.

"Gaspar," someone says. "Rod Gaspar."

"Who?"

"Rod Gaspar."

"Ron Gaspar?"

"No. Rod, Rod."

Pieper clears his throat and announces, "Playing right field, number seventeen, Rod Gaspar."

Pieper gives the name a sort of French pronunciation, as most people do. Gaspar himself pronounces his name as if it described a man trying to catch his breath.

Either way, Hodges hears the announcement, recognizes the name and knows he doesn't want Gaspar to replace Shamsky in the field. He moves out to home place and tells Bob Engel, the umpire, that he never officially inserted Gaspar into the lineup. Engel agrees, and Shamsky runs back out to right field. Gaspar trots back in, triggering a chain reaction.

Leo Durocher, the Chicago manager, trots out to the field, arguing that Gaspar must stay in the game, that once a man has been taken out of the lineup, he cannot return. The umpires explain the mix-up to Durocher, and the manager, appeased, crosses the infield on his way to his dugout. "How about a Schlitz, Leo?" calls Tom Seaver, from the pitcher's mound. Durocher has just finished a series of ten commercials for the brewery.

3:47 p.m.

Tom Seaver's wit is sharper than his curve today, which shows how much trouble he's having with the curve. His shoulder feels stiff. The Wrigley Field mound frustrates him. He keeps digging and kicking at it, trying to get a foothold in the hard dirt, but the mound won't yield. Only two fine fielding plays

169

by Ed Kranepool and Cleon Jones enable Seaver to get through the eighth inning with the score still 1–0.

3:50 p.m.

Bill Hands, who has allowed five hits up to now, retires Wayne Garrett and Ed Kranepool for the first two outs in the ninth inning. Then J. C. Martin comes up with his second hit, a single to left. With Phil Regan, his best relief pitcher, warming up in the bullpen, Leo Durocher walks out to the mound.

Gil Hodges sends Bud Harrelson in to run for Martin, and Donn Clendenon up to bat for Al Weis.

"How do you feel?" Durocher asks Hands.

"I've run out of gas," says Hands. "I'm finished."

Durocher signals for Regan, who throws sliders and sinking pitches and has already won eight games in relief this season. Regan is called "The Vulture," a nickname pinned on him by his Los Angeles teammates when he began making a habit of entering games in the late innings and picking up victories. In 1966, for the Dodgers, he picked up fourteen victories and only one defeat in relief. In his career, Regan is 7–0 against the Mets.

"I hated to leave with a shutout and all," Hands says later. "But I'm thinking that Clendenon is a good hitter who can hit the ball out of the park, and I'm tired. I hated to go, but I can't think about myself in that situation. I have to think about the ball club."

The Vulture gets a full count on Clendenon. On the next pitch, with Harrelson running, Clendenon gets the end of his bat on the ball and sends a soft line drive over second base. Glenn Beckert, the Cub second baseman, darts behind the bag, leaps and grabs the ball in the webbing of his glove. The game is over. The Cubs win, 1–0; they lead the Mets by five and a half games.

3:55 p.m.

As the last out is made, Ron Santo leaps high in the air and clicks his heels together, a victory dance he has perfected in recent weeks. Santo's leap delights the Bleacher Bums, who, unusually quiet all day, respond with cheers and grunts: "ABEEBEE! UNGOWA! CUB POWUH!" The Bum cheer is a direct steal, from, of all people, the Black Panthers.

170

4:00 p.m.

In the Met clubhouse, the players mill around a table holding pitchers of iced tea, circling aimlessly, slightly numbed by the defeat. "Why were the Bums so quiet today?" someone asks Tommie Agee, an expert on the subject.

"I think they were afraid they'd get us mad," says Agee, who went 0–for–4.

4:15 p.m.

"I love them," says Leo Durochers in the Cub clubhouse. "I love the Bleacher Bums."

Recently, when the Cubs played in St. Louis, a group of Bums followed them there and cornered Durocher in the Chase Park Plaza Hotel. "I bought ten guys and two girls a round of drinks," Durocher says. "Cost me $29.70. They drink double boilermakers."

4:16 p.m.

Dick Selma, the ex-Met who is scheduled to pitch against his old teammates tomorrow, is bouncing around the locker room, as excitable as ever. Often, he leads the Bleacher Bums in cheers.

Selma spots a New York sportswriter and grins. "Who's the pressure on now?" he says.

4:17 p.m.

"Yes, sir," says Leo Durocher, measuring the importance of his team's victory, "yes, sir, that was a World Series game."

4:20 p.m.

Tom Seaver sits by his locker, his head down, his shoulder and neck both stiff now. "That mound is ridiculous," he says, "It was like granite. It didn't do any good to scrape away the dirt because you just hit hard core."

"What about the pitch you threw to Billy Williams?" someone asks.

"It was a good pitch," Seaver says, "but Williams fought it off. He hit it off his fists and . . . and . . . well . . ." Seaver doesn't have to finish the sentence.

171

METS vs. CUBS at WRIGLEY FIELD DATE July 14, 1969

PLAYER	1	2	3	4	5	6	7	8	9	10	11	12	AB	R	H	RBI	2B	3B	HR	SO	SH	PO	A	E
AGEE													4	0	0	0	0	0	0	1			
BOSWELL													4	0	1	0	0	0	1	2	3	0	
JONES													4	0	1	0	0	0	1	5	0	0	
SHAMSKY													4	0	0	0	0	0	0	1	1	0	0
GARRETT													3	0	1	1	0	0	1	0	1	0	
KRANEPOOL													3	0	0	0	1	0	0	8	0	0	0
HARRELSON-p													4	0	0	0	0	0	0	4	0	0	0
MARTIN													1	0	0	0	0	0	0	0	0	0	
CLENDENON-1b													3	0	1	0	0	0	0	1	2	0	
WEIS													1	0	0	0	1	0	1	0	2	0	
SEAVER																							
TOTALS													31	0	6	3	0	0	5	21	7	0	

CUBS vs. METS AT WRIGLEY FIELD DATE JULY 14, 1969

PLAYER		1	2	3	4	5	6	7	8	9	10	11	12	AB	R	H				PO	A	E	
KESSINGER	6													3	1	1	0	0	1	0	2	0	2 base hits
BECKERT	4													4	0	1	0	0	0	0	5	2	0	3 base hits
WILLIAMS	9													3	0	2	0	1	0	1	0	0	Home runs
SANTO	5													3	0	0	0	0	1	0	2	2	0	Double plays
BANKS	3													3	0	1	0	0	0	8	1	0	Came to bats, out HANDS-3
HICKMAN	7													1	0	0	0	0	0	0	0	0	Struck out by HANDS-5
SMITH	7													2	0	0	0	0	0	0	0	0	Bases on balls, off HANDS-1½ REGAN-½
HUNDLEY	2													3	0	0	0	0	0	5	0	0	Earned runs off HANDS-0
QUALLS	8													3	0	0	0	0	0	6	0	0	Opponents runs off HANDS-6
REGAN - 9th	1													0	0	0	0	0	0	0	0	0	Wins pitcher HANDS-1
HANDS	1													3	0	0	0	0	2	0	0	0	
																							Winning pitcher HANDS 11-7
																							Losing pitcher SEAVER 14-4
																							Umpires DONATELLI, STEINER, STELLO, ENGEL
TOTALS														28	1	5	1	1	0	27	9	0	Score
																							Time of game 2:25

5:10 p.m.

As the Mets climb aboard their bus for the long ride back to the Executive House, Cub fans crowd around the windows, hollering the usual compliments. "The Cubs are gonna win the pennant," taunts one chubby youngster. "You'll see."

Bud Harrelson, the Met shortstop, is normally very polite, very friendly. But this is not a normal time. "Don't cash your checks yet, fat boy," Harrelson yells.

Eight

The Day Al Weis
Flexed his Muscles

TUESDAY
JULY 15, 1969

NATIONAL LEAGUE STANDINGS
Eastern Division

	W	L	PCT.	G.B.
Chicago	57	34	.622	—
New York	49	37	.570	5½
St. Louis	46	46	.500	11½
Pittsburgh	43	47	.478	13½
Philadelphia	38	49	.437	17
Montreal	28	61	.315	28

On July 15, 1963, the New York Mets had an excellent chance to match one of their all-time records. They had a double-header to play against the Houston Astros—then called the Colts—and if they could lose both games, they would extend their losing streak to seventeen straight, equaling the mark they set in their maiden season. The Mets, of course, were favored to keep their string alive.

But Carlton Willey, a pleasant New Englander who pitched and batted right-handed, ruined the Mets' losing streak, more with his bat than with his arm. In the second inning of the first game, Willey became the first Met pitcher ever to hit a grand-slam home run. His blow powered the Mets toward a 14–5 victory.

In the second game of the doubleheader, Roger Craig, the kind of pitcher you could trust to keep a losing streak going, enjoyed his thirteenth consecutive setback. Craig managed to keep his own personal losing streak going for eighteen games, still a Met record. "The losing doesn't bother me," Craig once reasoned. "It's the not winning that hurts."

Willey's victory was significant for the Mets in three ways: First, it raised the team's total of victories to thirty, a level they didn't reach until August 8 in 1962; second, it raised the team's total of victories at home to twenty-three, a level they never reached in 1962; third, it was the last time the Mets won a game on July 15. From Roger Craig's defeat in 1963 through a 500-foot home run by Philadelphia's Richie Allen in 1968, the Mets lost six straight games on July 15.

10:55 a.m.

On the team bus heading toward Wrigley Field, Gary Gentry, the New York Mets' rookie pitcher who is going to start against the Chicago Cubs this afternoon, admits that he is excited. "The last time I pitched against the Cubs," he says, "I told myself not to get excited. That was the wrong thing to do. I didn't get excited enough about the game."

Now Gentry is trying to psych himself into a state of angry tension. "I've spent all morning trying to tee myself off," he says. "I keep telling myself that these guys have beaten me twice this year. On my mistakes. That's enough to tee me off."

12:15 p.m.

Bud Harrelson walks into the Met dugout to check the lineup card posted by manager Gil Hodges. Harrelson has not started a single game since he returned from Camp Drum last Friday. He is not starting this one, either. Once again, Al Weis is listed at shortstop for the Mets. "Gil's saving me for the World Series," says Harrelson, with a smile.

12:25 p.m.

In batting practice, Jerry Grote, the Met catcher, hits a ball into the left-field bleachers. The Bleacher Bums throw the ball back on the outfield grass; they religiously do not accept balls hit to them by opposing batters.

The ball lands near Danny Frisella, who has been sprinting in the outfield with the other Met pitchers. Frisella throws the ball back into the stands. The Bums throw it out. Frisella throws it back.

A Burns security man, stationed among the Bums, yells at Frisella, "Don't you know we don't want any of them Met balls around here?" The Bums throw the ball over Frisella's head toward the infield. Ron Swoboda of the Mets picks it up and heaves it over the Bums and over the bleachers onto Waveland Avenue.

12:30 p.m.

On Waveland Avenue, a group of teenagers known as the Independence Park Ball Hawks have been waiting for a ball to fly out of Wrigley Field. When Ron Swoboda's throw hits the street, a fourteen-year-old boy named Goofy grabs the ball and starts to walk away. "Throw it back," chant the Bleacher Bums. "Throw it back."

But Goofy sells the ball to a friend, pot-bellied Marcelle Potvin, for a dollar. Then Potvin runs over to a souvenir stand. "How much you give me for this ball?" he asks the souvenir vendor.

"I'll give ya a buck an' a quarter," says the vendor.

Sold.

12:40 p.m.

Ken Boswell stands by the batting cage. The heat is intense, and sweat is trickling from his well-developed sideburns. "What did you do last night?" a reporter asks the Met infielder.

"I got so drunk the cabbie had to carry me up to my room," says Boswell, needling. Then, handing the reporter his bat, he says, "Here, you take this and I'll take your pen." The reporter refuses; he is afraid Boswell may drop his pen.

12:45 p.m.

Al Weis sits in the shade of the dugout. During the winter, his wife filled him with pasta and beer and he gained sixteen pounds, bringing his weight up to 170. At six feet tall, he was still skinny. Now, under the pressure of regular play and the summer heat, he is back down to 160. "I haven't been hitting the long ball yet this year," says Weis, flexing his muscles, "but I'll get my two or three homers."

In seven major-league seasons, Weis has hit exactly four home runs, none this year.

12:47 p.m.

As Jerry Koosman, the Met lefthander trots across the out-field, a foot-and-a-half-tall plastic doll bounces at his feet, a gift from the Bleacher Bums. Koosman picks the doll up and puts it inside his shirt, with just the head peeking out. He parades in front of the bleachers, tipping his hat graciously and bowing. The Bums applaud, and Koosman tosses the doll back into the stands.

12:55 p.m.

Outside Wrigley Field, the vendor sells the baseball he bought from Marcelle Potvin for $1.25 to a customer for $2.50. "A genuine souvenir of a Cubs game," says the vendor.

1:00 p.m.

One of the Bleacher Bums sounds a trumpet, and Ed Charles of the Mets, standing near the left-field bleachers, breaks into a little dance. "Might as well keep dancing," yells one of the yellow-helmeted Bums. "You can't play ball."

1:06 p.m.

A reporter asks Gil Hodges if the manager has given any thought to replacing Al Weis in the lineup with Bud Harrelson. "None," says Hodges, and walks away.

1:08 p.m.

Jerry Koosman relaxes on the Met bench, accepting congratulations from reporters and teammates. For the second straight year, he and Tom Seaver have been named to represent the Mets on the National League All-Star pitching staff.

"It cost me $500 to make that team," Koosman tells one writer, with a grin. "I couldn't have made it without the payoff."

"You sound like a man who doesn't have to pitch here," the writer says. Wrigley Field is not a comfortable park for left-handed pitchers.

"You know it," says Koosman. "There are a lot of teams in this league that I can't handle, and this is one of them. In fact, I don't belong in this league. I should be in some easier league."

1:10 p.m.

Gil Hodges analyzes Gary Gentry, his young pitcher, for the benefit of a Chicago writer. Gentry is warming up in the Met bullpen along the right-field line. "He had good schooling at that baseball college," says Hodges, referring to Arizona State, which is also the alma mater of Oakland's Reggie Jackson and Rick Monday. "And he knows his way around the mound. He fields his position, backs up plays, knows what to do with the ball when he gets it. But he makes mistakes with his pitches. And because he's got so much poise, you don't know why he does some of the things he does."

Hodges crosses his arms across his chest. "You forget he's so young," he says. "You're yelling on the bench for him to do this or do that. You tell him, 'You got the pitches, use them!' Then you realize that Gentry, and Nolan Ryan, they're just babies. They really haven't had the experience."

1:15 p.m.

Joe Pignatano, the Met coach, hollers to Ron Santo, the Cub third baseman, across the infield. "Watch," says Pignatano. Then he imitates the way Santo clicks his heels after a victory and yells, "Bush, that's real bush." Santo answers with the traditional obscene gesture.

180

1:20 p.m.

Wrigley Field, which looks like something out of an old news-reel about baseball before World War II, is packed to the last seat. There isn't even any standing room left. In front of the Met dugout, Yogi Berra and Joe Pignatano study the crowd.

"Hey, Joe," says Berra. "You know the last two words to the national anthem?"

"The brave," says Pignatano.

"Play ball!" cries Berra, and Pignatano laughs as if he were hearing the hoary joke for the first time.

1:27 p.m.

Gil Hodges carries the Met lineup card to home plate; Ron Santo, the Chicago captain, brings out the Cub lineup. After the umpires review the ground rules briefly, Santo turns to Hodges. "Tell Piggy," he says, "that the only reason I click my heels is because the fans will boo me if I don't."

Hodges, poker-faced, listens quietly. "You remind me of someone," he tells Santo. "You remind me of Tug McGraw. When he was young and immature and nervous, he used to jump up and down, too. He doesn't do it anymore."

1:30 p.m.

Dick Selma walks to the mound for the Chicago Cubs. Once, in the days before Tom Seaver and Jerry Koosman, Selma may have been the brightest pitching prospect in the Met organization. A graduate of California's Fresno High School—the same school that produced big-league pitchers Jim Maloney, Dick Ellsworth and, later, Seaver—Selma reached the major leagues in 1965, when he was only twenty-one years old. He won his first game against the Cardinals, then, in his second start, shut out the Braves, 1–0, in ten innings, striking out thirteen for a Met record.

Troubled by injuries and the lack of a good curve, Selma commuted back and forth between the Mets and the minors in 1966 and 1967, showing only occasional signs of brilliance. While he was with the Mets, he was one of their most amusing and outspoken players, so talkative and so intense that some of his teammates considered him "flaky," baseball talk for eccentric. Selma liked to explain that, at Fresno City College, he majored in body-and-fender work. "I took seven and a half credits of body and fender," he once said, "and I also studied first aid, introduction to physical education and the theory of baseball. They're what you'd call 'Mickey Mouse' courses."

Selma never quite fulfilled his promise as a Met. In 1968, after posting a dismal record in spring training, he got off to his strongest start, winning his first six decisions, tying the club record. Exactly a year ago today, he had an impressive 8–3 record, but when he lost seven of his last eight decisions, the Mets threw him into the expansion pool, and, on the first round, San Diego plucked him out. The Padres then traded him to Chicago.

As he gets ready for the first pitch of the game, Selma, still only twenty-five years old, owns a 9–3 record in 1969 and has struck out 104 men in 103 innings.

1:47 p.m.

With one man out in the top of the second inning and the score 0–0, Wayne Garrett singles to right field for the Mets. A daring young man seated in the middle of the Bleacher Bums promptly raises a small cardboard sign: LET'S GO, METS.

One of the officers of the Bums spots the Met fan, lifts a bullhorn to his mouth and shouts, "Commando squad, get ready."

Eight young Bums cluster together and, on command, push their way toward the offensive cardboard sign. One of them grabs it and rips it into little pieces. The daring Met fan does not argue. He sits silently, his hands folded on his lap.

2:01 p.m.

As the second inning ends, the game still scoreless, two young-sters run down the aisles in the left-field grandstand, display-ing a bedsheet covered by a slogan: LET'S GO, METS. A tor-rent of empty cups and an armada of flying garbage attack the Met fans. A couple of Wrigley Field ushers tell the youngsters they had better take their sign down, not because they may get hurt, but because overthrown garbage is bombarding the peo-ple in the left-field box seats.

2:03 p.m.

Al Weis, the skinny former White Sox infielder, singles to start the third inning. After Gary Gentry sacrifices Weis to

182

second, Dick Selma falls behind Tommie Agee, three balls, no strikes. From the dugout, Gil Hodges flashes a sign to Eddie Yost, the third-base coach, who relays the sign to Agee: Hit away if you get a good pitch.

Agee gets a good pitch and drives the ball deep into center field, up against the wall, 400 feet from home plate. Weis scores the first run of the game, and Agee races to third with a triple.

In the bleachers, a Met fan, stripped to the waist, waves his shirt wildly, signaling his pleasure. A Bleacher Bum takes a cup of Fresca and pours the full contents on the head of the Met fan, dampening his pleasure. The Met fan turns, his fists clenched, sees the rows and rows of Bleacher Bums and other Cub fans, and decides that he will let the Mets fight for him on the playing field.

2:09 p.m.

In the bottom of the third, Jimmy Qualls of the Cubs reaches second base on a single and a sacrifice, then, when Gary Gentry suffers a momentary mental lapse, steals third base. Don Kessinger's fly ball to center field brings Qualls home, and the score is tied, 1–1.

2:15 p.m.

As Art Shamsky starts the fourth inning with a single, two spectators positioned strategically close to a refreshment booth in the left-field grandstand begin waving orange-and-black Met banners. The two men—Jim Nickley and Bill Hazelwood—are renegades, native Chicagoans who work as freight handlers for Delta Air Lines; they switched their allegiance from the Cubs to the Mets in 1962 because, as Nickley says, "They try harder."

Nickley, a heavy-set, dark-haired Irishman wearing a bright green turtleneck and blue Bermuda shorts, and Hazlewood are celebrating each Met hit with a beer. Shamsky's single is an excuse for their fifth beer of the game.

2:18 p.m.

Dick Selma strikes out Wayne Garrett, his third strikeout in three and one-third innings.

2:20 p.m.

Ed Kranepool hits a long single to right field, so deep that even Art Shamsky is able to reach third base. Jim Nickley and Bill Hazelwood turn to their sixth beer in three and one-third innings.

2:22 p.m.

Dick Selma strikes out J. C. Martin, his fourth strikeout in three and two-thirds innings.

2:23 p.m.

Skinny Al Weis moves to the plate. In left field, a man named Wayne Kiska turns to Jim Nickley and Bill Hazelwood. The three men came to the game together, but Kiska, an unconverted Cub fan, is sitting a safe twenty feet away from his friends. "Hey!" he yells. "What do you think the little White Sox has-been will do?"

2:25 p.m.

Dick Selma gets two quick strikes on Al Weis, both on breaking pitches. Then Selma tries for the outside corner and barely misses. Weiss chokes up on his thirty-five-ounce bat. Selma stares in from the mound, and his catcher, Randy Hundley, flashes the curve-ball sign.

Selma shakes off the sign. He wants to go with his best pitch, his fast ball. Hundley now asks for the fast ball. Selma goes to his stretch, and first baseman Ernie Banks, who likes to shout at batters to confuse them, hollers, "Get that fast ball in there, now!"

The fast ball comes in, letter-high, over the middle of the plate. Weis swings and connects, and the ball sails out toward left field, over the Bleacher Bums, over the bleachers, into Waveland Avenue. Al Weis has struck his first home run of the 1969 season, his second in four years.

2:27 p.m.

Marcelle Potvin of the Independence Park Ball Hawks hears the roars and the groans inside Wrigley Field and gets ready for Al Weis's home run to bounce on Waveland Avenue

Potvin, who says he hasn't missed a Cub home game since he was expelled from school in May, immediately takes off after the ball. But the ball rolls right toward a seven-year-old youngster who is spending his first game on Waveland Avenue. The seven-year-old scoops up the home run. It is a good day for the little fellows.

2:28 p.m.

As Al Weis circles the bases, running his home run home, one thought occurs to him: "Be sure and touch every base."

After all, he doesn't do this sort of thing every day.

2:29 p.m.

In the left-field grandstand, Jim Nickley looks at his friend, Wayne Kiska, the Cub fan. "I don't know what the little White Sox has-been is gonna do," says Nickley, innocently. "Do you know what the little White Sox has-been is gonna do?"

Nickley shrugs off a shower of hot-dog rolls and faces the line of Cub fans by the refreshment stand. "What's the score?" he asks loudly. "Can anybody here tell me the score?"

The score is 4–1, and Nickley and his friend, Bill Hazelwood, start on their seventh beer in three and two-thirds innings.

2:30 p.m.

Dick Selma strikes out Gary Gentry, his fifth strikeout in four innings.

2:35 p.m.

With two out in the bottom of the fourth, Ernie Banks singles, the second Cub hit off Gary Gentry. As Banks stands on first base, Ed Kranepool turns to him. "You sure called the pitch on that one, Ernie," says Kranepool, referring to Banks' fast-ball shout on Al Weis's home run. "You'd make a helluva catcher."

Banks, for a change, says nothing. "When his team is losing," says Kranepool later, "Ernie's just like the rest of us. He's quiet."

2:38 p.m.

Fortunately for Jim Nickley and Bill Hazelwood, the Mets get only one hit in the fifth inning, a home run by Ken Boswell. New York leads, 5–1, and Dick Selma, the ex-Met, leaves the ball game.

3:05 p.m.

In the bottom of the sixth inning, with two men out and Ron Santo on first base, Tommie Agee charges a single by Ernie Banks and lets the ball skip by him to the wall. Santo scores, and the Cubs move within three runs, 5–2.

3:11 p.m.

Tommie Agee watches a called third strike and, disgusted by his strikeout and by his fielding error last inning, flings his bat away, nearly decapitating the on-deck batter, Ken Boswell, who ducks. Only Boswell's hands are iron, not his head.

3:15 p.m.

As Tommie Agee trots to his position in center field, the Bleacher Bums begin screaming at him for his tantrum. The Bums hoot. They dance on the railing. They clap. They wave Confederate flags. They call Agee "Hothead," "Busher" and considerably worse, perhaps giving him a little extra attention for his statement yesterday that the Bums were afraid to get the Mets angry. "They sure are in a different mood today," Agee tells himself.

3:30 p.m.

In the bottom of the eighth inning, Don Kessinger leads off with a single. Glenn Beckert steps up, and Ken Boswell, hoping for a double play, takes a few steps toward second base as Gary Gentry delivers the pitch. Beckert hits the ball straight up the middle, exactly where Boswell, contrary to reason, is playing. Boswell grabs the ball and starts a quick double play. "The dumb bastard," says one of the Cubs. "What the hell was he doing behind second base?"

Boswell's stupidity, enabling him to cut off a likely base hit, saves two runs, because the next batter, Billy Williams, drives Gentry's first pitch into the center-field stands.

186

Ron Santo moves to the plate, and Gentry gets two strikes on the clean-up hitter quickly. Gentry thinks about his next pitch. "Tom Seaver says that a real good pitcher like Bob Gibson or Juan Marichal doesn't waste pitches," Gentry explains later. "On oh-and-two, they go with their best."

Gentry goes with his best curve ball, over the plate, and Santo powers the ball over the fence and onto Waveland Avenue. The Cubs move within one run, 5–4.

"That was a dumb, dumb pitch I threw to Santo," Gentry says later. "I wasn't tired. I just made a mistake."

Gil Hodges decides he cannot risk another mistake by Gentry. The manager walks out to the mound and summons Ron Taylor, his most reliable relief pitcher, a thirty-one-year-old Canadian who failed to stick with Cleveland, St. Louis or Houston before he landed on the Mets.

A quiet college man, with a degree in electrical engineering and collections of stamps, jazz records and tropical fish, Taylor survives in the big leagues on intelligence, a good sinker and a sense of humor. "What do I have to work with?" he says. "Well, a little sinker, a slider that *backs up* some days and a change or two . . . you know, mediocre stuff."

Taylor reaches the mound, and Hodges flips him the ball. "You got a run," says the manager, "and nobody on."

Taylor gets Ernie Banks to pop up for the final out of the eighth inning.

3:47 p.m.

In the ninth inning, J. C. Martin singles, the Mets' first hit since Ken Boswell's home run. Jim Nickley and Bill Hazelwood thought they were never going to get another beer.

3:50 p.m.

The Cubs come up in the bottom of the ninth, for one more shot at Ron Taylor and his mediocre stuff.

On a two-and-two count to Willie Smith, a power hitter, Taylor throws his slider, the pitch that sometimes backs up. Smith swings and strikes out.

On an oh-and-two count to Randy Hundley, who also has power, Taylor delivers an inside pitch, a fast ball only by his own standards, Hundley swings and strikes out.

Jimmy Qualls, the man who spoiled Tom Seaver's perfect game, comes to bat. Qualls has two for three already today; he is batting .385 against the Mets. On Taylor's second pitch,

Qualls hits a ground ball to Ed Kranepool at first base. Taylor rushes toward first, Kranepool flips him the ball, Taylor steps on the bag and the game is over. The Mets win, 5–4. Wrigley Field is quiet. Even the Bleacher Bums are still.

3:59 p.m.

Al Weis, surrounded by reporters in the Met clubhouse, is reviewing out loud every single home run of his major-league career. The whole review takes him perhaps thirty seconds.

"Let's see," says Weis. "I hit my first one off Tommy John when he was pitching for Cleveland in 1964. Then the next one was off Dick Stigman in Minnesota. That was also in 1964. I hit one off Dave McNally of Baltimore in '65 and one off Cecil Upshaw last year. And now this one."

"You remember them all," says a reporter, with mock wonder.

"Why shouldn't I?" says Weis. "I spread them out. Once, when I hit a homer for the White Sox, I came into the dugout and all the guys were lying on the floor like they were dead or passed out from shock."

"Were you surprised when the ball went out today?" someone asks.

"I'm always surprised," says Weis.

4:10 p.m.

Leo Durocher, surrounded by reporters in the Cub clubhouse, puts a towel over his head. The reporters are asking him about Al Weis, and Durocher, who averaged 1.3 home runs himself for each of his nineteen major-league seasons, is unhappy. "Weis, Weis, Weis," he says. "Don't mention that name. Selma had to furnish the power. There had to be a tail wind. And he had to swing as hard as he could."

Durocher turns his attention to Dick Selma. "He wasn't struggling out there," the manager says. "He just wasn't thinking very well, I guess. It was lack of concentration. You got to think a little with a one-and-two pitch—throw a curve or a bad ball."

4:12 p.m.

"He hit my best pitch," says Dick Selma. "He hit my fast ball. He hit it out of the ball park. It's that simple."

188

4:14 p.m.

"I was in my protective stance," says Al Weis. "With two strikes on me, I choke up on the bat and just try to make contact."

No one has the heart to ask Weis what he tries to do the rest of the time. His lifetime major-league batting average is .224.

"I'd still like to break that home run up and have four singles for it," says Weis.

"Man," says Ed Charles, standing nearby, "not at that time. I wouldn't."

"Well," Weis admits, "I guess I wouldn't, either."

4:15 p.m.

"Are you ordering champagne for Al Weis?" a reporter asks Gil Hodges.

On May 25, 1968, when New York beat Atlanta, 9–1— when a Met infielder named Phil Linz, who is better known as a harmonica player (he once got fined by the Yankees for playing his harmonica on the team bus after a defeat) and as a saloonkeeper (of Mr. Laff's, a Manhattan hangout for athletes), got his first hit of the season, when Jerry Koosman got his first run-batted-in of the season and when Al Weis got his only home run of the season—Hodges ordered champagne for the three sluggers.

But now Hodges has only Weis to consider, not Linz, not Koosman. "If he hits another one tomorrow, in the same situation, with two men on," says the manager, generously, "I'll get him champagne."

4:16 p.m.

Joe Pignatano, the Met coach, is talking about his war of nerves with Leo Durocher. Early in the game, when Pignatano wandered out of the bullpen in right field and began waving a towel, Durocher complained to the umpires and they made Pignatano stop. "I was trying to aggravate Leo," says Pignatano, "and I guess I succeeded."

4:17 p.m.

"Did it bother you when Joe Pignatano started waving a towel?" a reporter asks Leo Durocher in the Chicago clubhouse.

"Pignatano couldn't do anything as a player," says Durocher, pleasantly. "Why should he worry me now?"

4:19 p.m.

Donn Clendenon, the tall, muscular slugger, reaches a hand into Al Weis's locker and pulls out a bottle of cologne. "This for home-run hitters?" he calls to Weis.

The skinny infielder grins.

Clendenon pours some cologne on his hand and rubs it into his face. "This enough?" he says.

4:20 p.m.

Ed Charles, perched in front of his locker, looks over at Donn Clendenon, who is thirty-four years old today. "Happy birthday," shouts Charles, who was thirty-six in April.

Clendenon scowls.

"Hey, Minnesota Fats," Charles calls to Rube Walker, using the coach's latest nickname. "Say happy birthday to Donn Clendenon."

"You're the Ernie Banks of the Mets," a reporter tells Charles, a tribute to the third baseman's good humor.

"No," says Harold Weissman, the Mets' public-relations director. "Banks is the Ed Charles of the Cubs."

4:28 p.m.

Ron Swoboda stands by the door to the clubhouse and confesses that he knew all along Al Weis would hit a home run. "I was just saying to myself, 'He might hit one,'" says Swoboda. "You can expect Selma to challenge a hitter—to throw his fast ball—and Weasel's a good fast-ball hitter."

4:30 p.m.

The other New York team loses the first game of a doubleheader and falls twenty-one and a half games out of first place.

4:35 p.m.

Skinny Al Weis, finally abandoned by the reporters, is getting dressed. "Let's face it," he says. "I'm no home-run hitter. I'm not even a hitter. I know my place on this club. I'm a fill-in man. I'm a substitute."

190

METS vs. CUBS AT WRIGLEY FIELD DATE JULY 15, 1969

PLAYER	1	2	3	4	5	6	7	8	9	10	11	12	AB	R	H				PO	A	E	
AGEE	8												4	1	2	0	1	0	6	0	0	1 item hits
BOSWELL	4												4	1	2	0	1	0	1	0	0	Home run: WEIS, BOSWELL
JONES	7												5	0	0	1	0	0	0	0	0	
GASPAR-rf	9												0	0	0	0	0	0	1	0	0	Double play: BOSWELL-WEIS-KRANEPOOL
SHAMSKY	9												3	1	1	0	0	0	0	0	0	Base on balls: off GENTRY-1
GARRETT	5												4	0	1	0	0	0	2	0	1	Struck out: by GENTRY-4
KRANEPOOL	3												4	1	1	0	0	0	6	2	0	Innings pitched by GENTRY-7⅓ TAYLOR-1⅔
MARTIN	2												4	0	1	0	0	0	2	0	0	Earned runs: off GENTRY-3
WEIS	6												4	1	2	0	3	0	1	3	0	Opponents' hits: off GENTRY-8
TAYLOR-ph	1												1	0	0	0	0	0	0	1	0	
GENTRY	1												2	0	0	0	0	0	1	2	0	
																						Passed balls:
																						Winning pitcher: GENTRY 9-1
																						Losing pitcher: SELMA 9-4
																						Umpires: DONATELLI, ENGEL, STELLO, STEINER
TOTALS													35	5	9	2	5	0	11	21	0	Score:
																						Time of game: 2:34

PLAYER	POS	1	2	3	4	5	6	7	8	9	10	11	12	AB	R	H	RBI	PO	A	E	
KESSINGER	6													3	0	1	0	1	2	0	WILLIAMS
BECKERT	4													4	0	0	0	2	1	0	SANTO
WILLIAMS	9													4	1	1	0	2	0	0	BANKS
SANTO	5													4	1	2	0	2	0		AGUIRRE
BANKS	3													4	0	1	0	7	0	0	
SMITH	7													3	0	1	0	2	0	0	
HUNDLEY	2													4	0	0	0	11	1	0	
QUALLS	8													4	1	1	0	1	0	0	
NYE - Sth	1													1	0	0	0	0	0	0	AGUIRRE
SELMA	1													1	0	0	0	0	1	0	
SPANGLER-Ph														1	0	0	0	0	0	0	
AGUIRRE	1													0	0	0	0	1	0		
TOTALS														32	4	8	3	16	2	0	

Time of game: 2:24

Nine

The Day
of the Hitters

WEDNESDAY
JULY 16, 1969

NATIONAL LEAGUE STANDINGS
Eastern Division

	W	L	PCT.	G.B.
Chicago	57	35	.620	—
New York	50	37	.575	4½
St. Louis	47	46	.505	10½
Pittsburgh	44	47	.484	12½
Philadelphia	38	50	.432	17
Montreal	28	62	.311	28

When the New York Mets awoke on the morning of July 16, 1968, they were in seventh place in the National League, higher than they had ever been so late in a baseball season. They were only seven games under .500, only seventeen games out of first place, new heights for them. They were the new Mets, the first New York team to be managed by Gil Hodges, and they were about to begin a four-game series against the Pittsburgh Pirates, who had lost ten straight games.

The new Mets had defeated the Pirates the first four times the two teams had met in 1968. The new Mets had Dick Selma, with a record of 8–3, set to pitch against the Pirates. The new Mets seemed to be on their way.

And on July 16, 1968, the new Mets played their new brand of ball. They didn't commit a single error. Cleon Jones slammed a single and a double. Ron Swoboda drove in two runs. Dick Selma limited the Pirates to a mere three hits in the first six innings.

There was, in fact, only one indication that the new Mets bore any resemblance to the old Mets: They lost the game. With two runs in the bottom of the seventh inning, Pittsburgh came from behind, scored a 3–2 victory, ended their ten-game losing streak and passed the Mets in the National League standings.

When the New York Mets went to sleep on the night of July 16, 1968, they were in ninth place in the National League. They had found the level they would maintain on the final day of the season.

11:25 a.m.

Don Cardwell, the starting pitcher for the New York Mets today, steps out of the team bus at Wrigley Field and heads toward the visiting team's clubhouse. Before he reaches the clubhouse, sweat is dripping off him. The temperature is already in the 90s.

Once, Cardwell pitched a no-hitter for the Chicago Cubs. But that was in 1960, when he was twenty-four years old and could throw hard all day. Now Cardwell is thirty-three, the oldest man on the Met pitching staff, nicknamed "Big Daddy" by his teammates, and he has completed only twelve games in three and a half years. (When he was twenty-five, he completed thirteen games in a single season.)

So far this season, Cardwell has started eleven games and has completed three. His record reflects his lack of endurance:

He has won three games and lost eight. The brutally hot weather is not on his side.

12:05 p.m.

After running half a wind-sprint across the outfield, Jerry Koosman, the Met pitcher, trots slowly to the dugout. "Man, it's hot," Ken Boswell, the infielder, calls to Koosman. "How'd you like to take batting practice for me?"

Koosman looks at Boswell scornfully. "You gotta be in shape," he says, "I could go another twenty laps out there." Then Koosman spreads out on the dugout floor, gasping for breath.

12:10 p.m.

In the Chicago clubhouse, Ferguson Jenkins, who is starting for the Cubs today, slouches in front of his locker, not even slightly worried about the heat. Jenkins, the victim of the Mets' ninth-inning rally last week, is twenty-five years old and incredibly durable. He completed twenty games in 1967 and twenty in 1968; he has completed fourteen games already this season, more than Don Cardwell has completed in three and a half seasons.

Jenkins is so sure of his stamina, in fact, that, at the start of each inning, he sprints to the pitcher's mound.

12:15 p.m.

Tommie Agee emerges from the Met dugout and feels the full force of the sunshine. "I want to see if Fergie runs out to the mound today," says Agee.

12:30 p.m.

As Ken Boswell steps into the batting cage, he manages a smile. "I'm gonna get *two* bloops off Jenkins today," he says, recalling his pop-fly double that started the Met uprising last week.

Boswell takes a few cuts and steps out of the cage, drenched with perspiration. "That Jenkins doesn't even sweat," Art Shamsky says to Boswell. "He wears long sleeves on days like this."

Boswell shakes his head. "I don't think I can last through infield drill," he says. Then he looks at his soaked uniform and adds, "Must be all that bourbon coming out."

196

12:35 p.m.

In the packed left-field bleachers, one of the cheerleaders among the Bleacher Bums picks up a bullhorn and conducts the Bums in a chant: "The Mets are number two! The Mets are number two! The Mets are number two!"

12:40 p.m.

Lou Boudreau, the former All-Star shortstop for the Boston Red Sox and Cleveland Indians and now a sportscaster for the Cubs, is preparing to interview Yogi Berra near the box seats behind home plate. When Boudreau announced yesterday that his guest today would be "The Singing Dago," he inspired dozens of phone calls, few of them complimentary, from his Italian listeners.

Yogi doesn't understand the fuss. "Hell, Lou's right," says Berra. "I *was* always singing to him when he came to bat."

Boudreau begins the interview with a neat, brief apology, pacifying his Italian audience. Berra says nothing that could offend anyone except English teachers.

12:42 p.m.

On his way to the Met dugout, Gil Hodges is hailed by Francis X. Smith, the president of the New York City Council. Smith has come to Chicago to see the Mets play and to umpire a softball game between Republican and Democratic members of the Chicago City Council.

Smith, sitting in a box seat near the Met dugout, is both a good Met fan and a good politician. He shakes hands with Hodges and hands the manager a tie-clip, a symbolic key to the City of New York. Hodges fastens the clip to the lapel of his baseball shirt.

"I live only ten minutes from Shea Stadium," says Smith. "I never miss a home game."

"Doesn't it bother Mayor Lindsay that you take time off to go to the ball park?" a reporter asks the City Council president, who is running for re-election.

John Lindsay and Francis Smith are on opposite teams in New York politics. Lindsay is also running for re-election.

"The Mayor didn't even make opening day at Shea Stadium," says Smith, bidding for the baseball vote.

12:45 p.m.

Don Cardwell waits for his turn in the batting cage. Six-foot-four and 220 pounds, Cardwell may be the most powerful of the Mets. He has hit more home runs in the major leagues than all the other Met pitchers combined; in fact, he has hit exactly as many home runs in the major leagues as five Met infielders combined—Bud Harrelson, Wayne Garrett, Ken Boswell, Bobby Pfeil and Al Weis. Cardwell picked up his fifteenth big-league home run early this season; he is batting .222 for the year.

"I had my stroke going for a while," says Cardwell. "I went three-for-three one game. Then the stroke went away. Today would be a good day to get it back. Look at that flag in center field. The wind's blowing straight out."

Cardwell smiles, but he knows that if the wind is good for his hitting, it is terrible for his pitching. "The Cubs hit good pitches right out of here," he says. "If you get a pitch up high, any guy has a chance to hit the ball out. With Ernie Banks, even if you pitch him down and away, he can still lift it into the left-field stands."

The big pitcher shakes his head and steps into the batting cage. Both the wind and the heat are operating against him. "My luck is bound to change any day now," he says.

12:50 p.m.

Ed Charles has staked out the coolest seat in the Met dugout, at the end of the bench near the tunnel leading to the clubhouse. "I feel sorry for you guys," Charles hollers to the starting infielders running out for their pre-game drill. "You really got to love the game to play today. Let's see some hustle out there."

1:00 p.m.

A female Bleacher Bum grabs the bullhorn. "Okay," she yells to the rest of the bleachers crowd. "We're all gonna learn the fight song now. You ready? Let's go: 'Hey, Hey, Holy Mackerel . . .' "

1:10 p.m.

Don Cardwell begins warming up in the Met bullpen. In the minor leagues, Cardwell studied under a former pitcher named

Don "The Wizard" Osborn, a soft-spoken man who liked to instruct his charges in the more exotic deliveries. For instance, Osborn taught the razor ball, the fingernail ball, the belt-buckle ball, the pine-tar ball, the slippery-elm ball, the tobacco-juice ball, the chewing-gum ball and the old reliable spit ball, each delivery guaranteed to make the baseball take spectacular dips and twists and each delivery outlawed by the rules of baseball.

Cardwell's own theory of pitching is simple: "Keep the ball down, with a sinker here, a slider there, run the ball in—and look out!"

The veteran righthander has one glaring weakness in his style. "When I start throwing below three-quarters overhand," he says, "my sinker straightens out, my slider flattens out and I tend to throw everything high. I can't really tell myself when I'm doing it." Usually, when Cardwell's motion starts to slip, either Gil Hodges or Rube Walker tells him what's happening. "If they don't get to me first," he says, "the hitters have a way of letting me know."

1:33 p.m.

Ferguson Jenkins sprints out to the pitcher's mound.

1:34 p.m.

Behind home plate, umpire Augie Donatelli, who has rolled his trousers up to the knee to beat the heat, signals for play to begin.

1:35 p.m.

In the left-field bleachers, a group of Bums hold up a sign: FERGIE'S NUMBER ONE TO US.

The reference is to the fact that Red Schoendienst, the St. Louis manager who is managing the National League All-Star team, has not named Ferguson Jenkins—or any other Cub—to his pitching staff.

Jenkins' omission has angered both the Cub fans and the Cub players, particularly Ron Santo, who has started sniping at Schoendienst in his daily column in the *Chicago Daily News*.

Chicago's fury seems justified: Jenkins has a record of 12–6, with 156 strikeouts, the most in the National League.

1:36 p.m.

Tommie Agee slams Ferguson Jenkins' first pitch past third base for a double. Ken Boswell, the bloop specialist, bloops a single into right field. The Mets lead, 1–0, and in the upper stands, a teenager wearing a Mets button cheers and hugs his blonde girl friend.

Cleon Jones singles up the middle, sending Boswell to third, then steals second to put two runs in scoring position.

Jenkins is getting heat, but not from the sun. He throws a fast ball past Art Shamsky for his 157th strikeout of the year.

1:41 p.m.

Leo Durocher trots out to the mound. The manager and his ace pitcher decide to walk Wayne Garrett to load the bases. The strategy is perfect, and, from a New York viewpoint, so are the results. When Ed Kranepool gets an infield single and J. C. Martin drops a single into left field, the Mets lead, 4–0.

Al Weis, the home-run hitter yesterday, then reverts to form and Don Cardwell wastes his power, and they become Ferguson Jenkins' 158th and 159th strikeouts of 1969.

As the inning ends, the young man with the Mets button and his blonde friend leave their seats, walk halfway down a ramp leading to a refreshment stand and, while the Mets trot out to the field holding a four-run lead, start holding each other.

1:54 p.m.

Don Cardwell, pouring sweat, gives up a single and hits a Cub batter in the bottom of the first inning, but a double play and a fine catch by Cleon Jones, timing his move just right, get the veteran pitcher through the inning without damage. In the upper deck, the boy and the blonde, timing their moves just right, hustle back to their seats as the Mets hustle in to hit.

1:59 p.m.

Tommie Agee leads off for the second straight inning. This time he doesn't settle for a double. He hits a home run, a line drive into the left-field bleachers.

The Bleacher Bums, as usual, fearful that they will be contaminated by any ball hit by an opponent, toss Agee's home-run ball back onto the field. The run counts, anyway. New York leads, 5–0, and Agee, who hit five home runs all last season, now has sixteen in 1969.

2:01 p.m.

Cub coach Verlon "Rube" Walker shuffles to the mound and summons Hank Aguirre, a thirty-seven-year-old left-handed junk-ball pitcher, to replace Ferguson Jenkins. The durable Canadian has lasted only one official inning. "I don't know what was wrong," Jenkins says later. "I wasn't in there long enough to find out."

The sprinting pitcher now walks slowly off the field.

2:05 p.m.

Before Hank Aguirre can retire the side, singles by Cleon Jones and Art Shamsky, plus an infield grounder, enable the Mets to lengthen their lead to 6–0. As soon as the inning ends, the young couple in the upper deck retreat to the privacy of the ramp. They don't waste their time watching the Cubs hit.

2:13 p.m.

The Bleacher Bums, stung by Tommie Agee's home run, begin abusing the Met center fielder. The Bums, trailing 6–0, are not in their best form. "Hey, Agee, I hear you sleep with Al Lopez," a reference to Agee's former White Sox manager, is the most vile insult the Bums can manage.

2:14 p.m.

Ernie Banks leads off against his old teammate, Don Cardwell, with a double, and after one out, Randy Hundley singles Banks home. After a second out, Hank Aguirre walks up to the plate, the perfect batter in this situation, from Cardwell's point of view. As a relief pitcher, Aguirre doesn't get to bat very often. He gets on base even more rarely. He has hit safely only twice in the past three years.

Now Aguirre pops up meekly to short right field. Tommie Agee cuts over, Art Shamsky lumbers in, and Ken Boswell pedals back. At the last second, Agee brakes, Shamsky halts and Boswell retreats. The ball drops for a single, putting runners on first and third.

Cardwell isn't surprised. When he pitches, even when he

pitches very well, he seems to inspire the Mets to field poorly and hit worse. Generally, Cardwell gets about as much support as the Bay of Pigs invasion received.

Naturally, Don Kessinger then singles off Boswell's iron glove, Glenn Beckert loops a single in front of Cleon Jones, the Cubs are back in the game, 6–3, and Cardwell is out.

If anyone had told him before the game that he would last two-thirds of an inning longer than Ferguson Jenkins, Cardwell probably would have been happy. He isn't happy now.

2:24 p.m.

Jim McAndrew, the psychology major from Iowa, comes in to pitch for the Mets, and Billy Williams welcomes him with a single, bringing the Cubs within two runs, 6–4.

Finally, McAndrew gets the third out—sixteen minutes after the Cubs came to bat—and, in the upper deck, the romantic teenagers return to their seats. If the rally had lasted another batter or two, they might never have gotten back to the game.

2:34 p.m.

As the Mets fail to score in the top of the third inning, a college student in the left-field stands hoists a homemade sign: LET'S GO, METS. The phrase isn't very original, but the background for it is. Steve Olsen, a graduate student in physics at the University of Wisconsin, has written the Mets slogan on computer-output paper.

The Cub fans sitting around him show their admiration for Olsen's ingenuity by showering him with paper cups and hot-dog rolls. "Some of these fans," says Olsen, turning to a young lady sitting next to him, "should be out there pitching for the Cubs."

2:37 p.m.

In the bottom of the third inning, Ernie Banks singles, Willie Smith singles and Jim McAndrew departs, having pitched two-thirds of an inning less than Ferguson Jenkins, one and one-third innings less than Don Cardwell.

Gil Hodges calls in Cal Koonce to replace McAndrew. Koonce is normally the Mets' "short man," used to pitch only two or three innings at the end of a game, but with Tug McGraw still on Marine duty, Hodges has little choice.

The third inning is not a total stranger to Koonce. As recently as three years ago, he was basically a starting pitcher. When he finished a tour in the minor leagues and returned to the Cubs early in the 1966 season, Leo Durocher turned him into a relief pitcher. Then, late in the 1967 season, Durocher gave up on him and turned him into a Met. He was, in 1968, with an earned run average of 2.41, the first truly effective relief pitcher the New York Mets ever owned. In his first thirteen appearances of the year, he didn't allow a single earned run; he finished the season with six consecutive victories.

Now, Koonce does about as good a job as Hodges, or anyone else, could expect. He retires three straight hitters; still, with a sacrifice bunt followed by a sacrifice fly, the Cubs score another run and cut the Mets' lead to 6–5.

The upper-deck lovers leave their hideaway ramp and decide to watch the rest of the game from their seats. The traffic is getting too heavy on the ramp. Besides, the game itself is pretty exciting by now.

3:04 p.m.

As J. C. Martin comes to bat in the fourth inning, with the bases loaded and two men out, Al Weis kneels in the on-deck circle. From the nearby stands, someone yells, "I don't believe it, Weis. I still don't believe it. You can't hit a home run."

The skinny infielder doesn't even turn around. Martin strikes out, and Weis trots out to shortstop.

3:16 p.m.

The score is still 6–5, and Al Weis leads off for the Mets. He is facing a new Cub pitcher, Rich Nye, who, unlike Dick Selma yesterday, does not challenge Weis with a fast ball. Nye throws a curve, and the curve hangs, and Weis swings, connects and drives the ball deep into left-center field.

"Oh, no!" says Jack Brickhouse, who is broadcasting the game to Chicagoans. "Not again!"

Again.

Weis's blow lands in the bleachers. He has now hit as many home runs in two days as he hit in the previous four and a half years.

The Mets lead, 7–5.

3:42 p.m.

In the top of the seventh inning, Al Weis kneels once more in the on-deck circle. The same voice that had taunted him earlier floats out of the stands: "All right, Weis, I believe you. I believe you. Stop already."

Weis grounds out to shortstop.

3:46 p.m.

The Bums are restless in the left-field bleachers. Some of them are no longer paying any attention to the game, simply screaming and drinking. Ron Grousl, the leader of the Bums, is making the most noise.

"Why don't you sit down and watch the game?" a bold young fan yells at Grousl.

"Why don't you shut up?" Grousl shouts back. Then Grousl and a few of his friends charge the young fan, knocking over a vendor and splattering Cokes on the people nearby.

A security guard, a short, thin man wearing sunglasses tucked into his sideburns, carrying a can of Mace upside-down in its holster, moves to break up the scuffle. The guard, an honorary Bum, settles the matter by leading away the young fan who wanted to watch the game.

4:00 p.m.

With two men out in the top of the eighth, Cleon Jones hits a hard ground ball to third base. Ron Santo scoops up the ball and pegs it into the dirt in front of Ernie Banks. Jones is safe on Santo's error. "Hey, Santo," someone hollers from the Met bench, "you gonna write yourself up in your column saying how beautiful you are now?"

4:02 p.m.

Art Shamsky steps up to the plate. He is a perfect symbol of the Mets' sudden success. In three seasons as an extra outfielder with the Cincinnati Reds, from 1965 through 1967, Shamsky, with his slow legs and level left-handed swing, enjoyed a total of forty-eight hours of brilliance. On August 12, 1966, he hit three home runs in a row. He was benched the next day, but on August 14, as a pinch-hitter, he tied the major-league record for four consecutive home runs.

But, otherwise, Shamsky compiled a mediocre .231 lifetime average, only a modest reputation as a power hitter and a history of self-doubt. "Sometimes I know I'm as good a hitter as anybody," he once said, "and then I'm not. I don't know why." In 1968, his first years with the Mets, he did little to nourish his self-respect. He hit .238.

This spring Shamsky hit bottom. Catching grounders thrown at him during training camp, Shamsky suddenly felt his back go. "It was like somebody had taken a gun and shot me," he says. "I felt this sharp pain shoot all the way down my leg." Pills and shots didn't help, and doctors warned Shamsky that he might never play ball again. "I thought I might be paralyzed for life," he says. "You start thinking about those things."

When the season began, Shamsky, who had been convalescing at home, flew to New York and pleaded for a spot on the team. His back felt better, he said. The Mets told him to go down to the Tidewater farm team and play himself into shape. Shamsky was tempted to quit baseball, but he put aside his pride and reported to Tidewater. After two and a half weeks in Virginia, he rejoined the Mets.

Since then, Shamsky, with a batting average of .346, has become the Mets' second most consistent hitter. Duck-footed, used only against right-handed pitchers, he is one of the reasons Wrigley Field is full today.

Ted Abernathy, the right-handed submarine pitcher, is now pitching for the Cubs. He underhands Shamsky a low fast ball. Shamsky is a low fast-ball hitter. He swings, and the ball travels high in the air towards left-center field. The wind catches the ball and carries it into the sea of yellow helmets in the bleachers. The Mets lead, 9–5.

4:04 p.m.

The home-run ball struck by Art Shamsky bounced off a few seats and into the hands of an eleven-year-old Cub fan. Immediately, the Bleacher Bums go into their chant: "Toss it back. Toss it back. Toss it back." The youngster wants to keep his souvenir, but the Bums keep shouting.

Finally, the young fan reluctantly hands the ball to a Bum who hurls it toward second base, interrupting play.

4:10 p.m.

Cal Koonce has held the Cubs through five innings without allowing an earned run, and, in the bottom of the eighth, Gil

Hodges rewards him with a rest. Ron Taylor comes in and retires the Cubs, one-two-three.

4:18 p.m.

J. C. Martin stands on first base with a single. The Mets are playing hit-and-run. Martin heads for second, and Al Weis fouls the ball off. Again Martin goes, and again Weis fouls the ball off. It is difficult for any catcher to sprint even on a cool day after eight innings behind the plate. Martin is sprinting through an inferno.

Warming up Jack DiLauro in the bullpen, Jerry Grote begins to feel dizzy and sits down. "Everything started to get a little blurry," he says later.

4:25 p.m.

The less optimistic Cub fans in the crowd of 36,795 paying customers begin filing out of Wrigley Field. For the three games in Chicago, the paid attendance has totaled more than 112,000, making the Met-Cub series the biggest in the city since the Dodgers and the White Sox met in the World Series ten years ago. The average paid attendance for the six games between the Mets and the Cubs in the past nine days is an impressive, and immensely profitable, 39,000 a game.

4:30 p.m.

With one out in the bottom of the ninth inning, Chicago has runners on first and second, and the most dangerous Cubs, Billy Williams and Ron Santo, are coming to bat. Ron Taylor, the Canadian engineer, bears down.

First, Taylor gets Williams on a pop fly to second base. Then he faces Santo, the third baseman, columnist and heel-clicking cheer-leader. Taylor throws a slider, and Santo half swings, half holds up. He lifts a tiny fly ball toward second base. Ken Boswell grabs the ball and the game is over. The Mets win, 9–5, their sixth victory in the critical nine games, their fourth victory in six games against Chicago.

Tom Seaver, one of the first Mets out of the dugout to congratulate Taylor, sprints to the mound and, halfway there, takes a small hop in the air and, ever so gently, clicks his heels together.

4:38 p.m.

As the Mets trot up the stairs to their clubhouse, a group of youngsters crowd around a nearby wire fence. "You're still worse than the Cubs," shouts one heckler.

Ron Swoboda turns. "Eat your heart out," he says.

4:39 p.m.

The Bleacher Bums are still littering the outfield, not with garbage this time, but with their ripped-up signs and banners in praise of the Cubs. At the rear of the bleachers, a few of the Bums are dismantling the CUB POWER banner they created out of paper cups woven into the left-field fence.

4:40 p.m.

The Met clubhouse is noisy and joyful. "I have a press release," Tom Seaver shouts. "Al Weis is only 483 years behind Babe Ruth."

Someone asks Seaver about his heel-clicking act, and the pitcher grins and says, "Oh, you noticed that? It was just a little kick, a small dig."

4:41 p.m.

A reporter asks Gil Hodges, who generally doesn't approve of any fooling around on the field, if Tom Seaver's leap bothered him. "Seaver deserved it," says Hodges. "I saw him waiting so patiently in the dugout."

4:42 p.m.

A few of the Mets are teasing Al Weis because his home run today merely carried into the bleachers, not out of the ball park like yesterday's drive. "Weis has lost a little power," says Gil Hodges, with a straight face.

"I don't know why it didn't go out," Weis counters. "It had enough power to go out." For the second straight day, he shows off his muscles.

The manager had not ordered champagne for Weis, presumably because his home run today came with the bases empty.

207

4:43 p.m.

"Hey," yells one of the Mets, above the roar of the clubhouse, "wait'll we get 'em in Wrigley Field next week!"

Ron Santo had said the same thing after the series in Shea Stadium last week, and now all the Mets laugh.

4:44 p.m.

In the Chicago clubhouse, a small pack of New York reporters peck away at Leo Durocher. Is he worried about the Mets? Are they the main threat to his pennant chances? How important was today's game?

"Just another ball game," says Durocher. "Don't forget who's in first place."

"Are the Mets for real?" someone asks.

"Are you asking me to dismiss the Cardinals, the Pirates, the Phillies—even Montreal?" says Durocher. "All I ask you is: Who's in first place?"

"You are," says a reporter.

"That's all," says Durocher.

4:45 p.m.

Gil Hodges walks over to the soft-drink cooler in the middle of the Met locker room and picks up a telegram. It reads: ALL NEW YORK WISHES YOU AND THE METS BEST OF LUCK IN THE SECOND CITY. LET'S GO, METS.

The telegram is signed: Mayor John V. Lindsay.

4:50 p.m.

Someone asks Bud Harrelson, who has hardly played since his return from military duty, what's been happening on the Met bench. "I don't pay much attention," says Harrelson. "I'm too busy helping Gil manage."

5:02 p.m.

In a corner of the Chicago clubhouse, Ron Santo sits, his feet propped up on a box filled with letters to him from Cub fans. A good percentage of the letters this week have not been favorable. "The Mets beat us," says Santo, still a bit dazed. "They beat us. You have to give them credit for that. Two out

208

of three in our park." Santo shakes his head. "I still don't believe it," he says.

5:09 p.m.

In the Met clubhouse, Ron Taylor, the relief pitcher turns to a reporter. "Are the nine crucial days over yet?" he asks, mocking the phrase used to describe the games with the Cubs and the Montreal Expos.

"Not till midnight," says the reporter.

"Then all that's left," replies Taylor, "is the crucial plane ride to Montreal."

5:10 p.m.

J. C. Martin is sitting in front of his locker, a blank look on his face. He has barely moved since he entered the clubhouse. "You better go in and see the trainer," Don Cardwell suggests.

5:13 p.m.

J. C. Martin walks into the trainer's room. "I've got chills," he tells Gus Mauch. "And I'm starting to get pains in my chest."

Mauch immediately brings out a stretcher and puts Martin on it. Martin is wheeled out of the clubhouse and taken, by ambulance, to Wesley Memorial Hospital, for a check-up to find out whether he might have suffered a heart attack.

5:25 p.m.

At Wesley Memorial Hospital, a doctor determines that J. C. Martin is suffering only from heat prostration. The doctor injects a saline solution into Martin's right wrist and dispatches the catcher to rejoin his teammates for the crucial plane ride to Montreal.

6:50 p.m.

Aboard the sweltering team bus heading toward O'Hare Airport, Cal Koonce, the pitching hero of the day, displays a poem he has written to celebrate the victory:

> "The Cubs have Kessinger to Beckert to Banks
> Their ability carries no shame,
> But for general purposes I would just as soon have
> Weis to Boswell to Krane.

Koonce pitches better than he rhymes.

METS vs. CUBS AT WRIGLEY FIELD DATE July 16, 1969

PLAYER	1	2	3	4	5	6	7	8	9	10	11	12	AB	R	H	PO	A	E
AGEE	8												5	2	2	1	0	0
BOSWELL	4												5	1	2	0	6	5
JONES	7												5	3	2	0	0	0
TAYLOR - 9th	1												0	0	0	0	1	1
SHAMSKY	9												5	1	3	0	2	0
GARRETT	5												3	1	0	2	1	0
CLENDENON - 2b	3												3	0	0	0	2	0
KRANEPOOL	3												2	0	1	0	5	0
MARTIN	2												5	0	2	0	1	0
WEIS	6												5	1	1	0	2	4
McANDREW	1												0	0	0	0	0	0
CARDWELL	1												1	0	0	0	0	0
KOONCE - 3rd	1												0	0	0	0	0	0
GASPAR - 8th	9												1	0	0	0	0	0
TOTALS													42	9	14	39	16	0

Time of game — 3:00

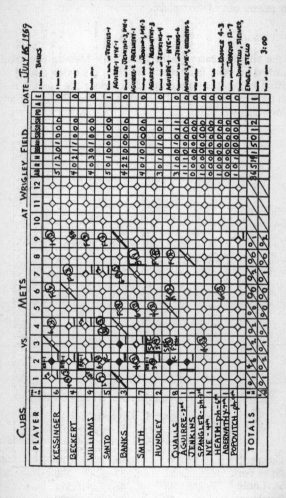

CUBS vs METS AT WRIGLEY FIELD DATE JULY 16, 1969

211

9:34 p.m.

The other New York team loses a single game and falls twenty-two games out of first place.

9:45 p.m.

In the airplane carrying the New York Mets to Montreal, Ed Charles, the poet laureate of the club, is singing a song he has written to commemorate the Cub series. The song is a variation on "The Sidewalks of New York," and Charles thoroughly enjoys his own lyrics:

> "East side, west side,
> The fans are feeling gay.
> After seven long, long years,
> The Mets are on their way.
>
> "South side, north side,
> The word is going round.
> When October rolls around,
> The Mets will win the crown.
>
> "East side, west side,
> The fans are feeling gay.
> After seven long, long years,
> The Mets are on their way. . . ."

JULY 17, 1969
NATIONAL LEAGUE STANDINGS
Eastern Division

	W	L	PCT.	G.B.
Chicago	57	36	.613	—
New York	51	37	.580	3½
St. Louis	48	46	.511	9½
Pittsburgh	45	47	.489	11½
Philadelphia	38	51	.427	17
Montreal	28	63	.308	28

TEN

The Year the Mets
Lost Last Place

On the morning of July 17, 1969, the New York Mets awoke and found that they had survived the first nine-day crisis of their existence. They had done better than survive. They had flourished. They were securely in second place in the Eastern Division of the National League, only three and a half games behind the Chicago Cubs, six full games ahead of the St. Louis Cardinals, the defending National League champions.

The Mets were unquestionably in a pleasant position, but with almost half the season still to play, no one was quite ready to predict a pennant for them. With their hitters, they could without warning, fall into the worst batting slump in baesball history, and hardly anyone would notice the difference. Any day, their young pitchers could be betrayed, either by their own arms or by the fielders behind them, and not one of the Mets regulars had any experience at playing under pressure—unless you consider the 1968 fight for ninth place a critical battle.

On the morning of July 17, two American astronauts were on their way to walk on the moon, but the Mets, and their followers, had far less lofty goals. The realists among them probably would have settled, right then, for a guarantee of second place; first place seemed too much to ask only a year after ninth place. By the end of July, the Cubs were six games in front of the Mets, and the days ahead looked treacherous for the New Yorkers. In the month of August, they were scheduled to face Atlanta, San Francisco, Los Angeles, Cincinnati, and Houston, the tough teams of the Western Division, and even an optimist would have predicted nothing much better than a .500 month.

For thirteen days, August was a wicked month for the Mets. After three straight defeats in the Houston Astrodome, a terrain that seems to terrify the Mets, the New Yorkers owned an August record of 7–8, and they trailed Chicago by nine and a half games. Their situation appeared hopeless; they were too far behind with too little time to go. The realists feared that the Mets were charging toward fourth place, behind St. Louis and Pittsburgh.

Then, suddenly, against all logic, the Mets caught fire. They swept two consecutive doubleheaders from the San Diego Padres, and everything began to go their way—pitching, hitting, and luck. They won fourteen of their last sixteen games in August, finishing the month with a 21–10 record, the most successful month in their history. On the morning of September 1, the Mets stood only four games behind the sagging Chicago Cubs.

If the Mets were truly amazing in August, they were absolutely incredible in September. They roared, and Chicago reeled. While the Mets were ripping off a ten-game winning streak in the early part of the month, the Cubs were suffering through an eight-game losing streak. Unbelievably, ridiculously, beautifully, on September 10, by winning the first game of a twi-night doubleheader (and later the second game) against the bilingual Montreal Expos, the Mets, of all teams, jumped into first place in the National League's Eastern Division. They had gained ten games on the Cubs in less than a month. "LOOK WHO'S NO. 1" proclaimed the scoreboard at Shea Stadium, and most viewers blinked at least twice before they could believe it.

In the month of September, in the eighth year of their existence, the Mets performed miracles daily. One day, for instance, they played a doubleheader against the hard-hitting Pittsburgh Pirates and won each game by the unlikely score of 1–0. More unlikely, in each game the starting Mets pitcher drove in the only run. Most unlikely, in one of the games the starting Mets pitcher was Jerry Koosman. When Koosman drove in a run, everyone who knew anything about baseball knew that something more than skill was operating on the side of the Mets. A few days later the Mets established an all-time major-league record by striking out nineteen times against Steve Carleton of the St. Louis Cardinals; in the same game, the Mets committed four fielding errors. Their hitting and their defense collapsed simultaneously, yet, absurdly, they still won the game, 4–3, because Ron Swoboda, recapturing his power swing, drove two home runs over the fence, each with a Met on base.

Even on the rare occasions when the Mets lost in September, they managed to lose sublimely—once to a no-hitter thrown by Bob Moose of the Pittsburgh Pirates.

Exactly two weeks to the day after they tasted first place for the first time—on September 24, when young Gary Gentry shut out the St. Louis Cardinals, 6–0, at Shea Stadium—the Mets clinched the division championship. Afterward, in a locker room scene of pure joy, the Mets ran through fifteen cases of champagne. They hardly drank a drop; most of them

216

looked too young. They celebrated by pouring the stuff over each other's heads.

The Mets finished September with a magnificent mark for the month of 23–7, including one stretch of fourteen victories in fifteen games. The Cubs finished September with a record of 9–17, including one stretch of eleven defeats in twelve games.

On October 1, 1969, the Mets returned to Wrigley Field—their first visit to Chicago since July 16—for the final two games of the regular season against the Cubs. "It would be great," Ed Kranepool had said back on July 9, "to go into Chicago the last two games of the season with a three-game lead and tell Ernie Banks, 'It's a great day to play two, Ernie.'"

The Mets didn't go into Chicago with a three-game lead; they went in with an eight-game lead. They had gained seventeen and a half games on the Cubs in a little more than seven weeks. But Kranepool did not needle Ernie Banks. Most of the Mets, in fact, seemed to feel a little sorry for Banks, who had been waiting so long, and so cheerfully, for a chance to play in a World Series.

But none of the Mets showed any sympathy for Leo Durocher, or for Ron Santo, or for Chicago's Bleacher Bums, subdued, almost silenced by their club's collapse. The Mets split the final games in Chicago, completing the season with precisely 100 victories and with 62 defeats, a stunning .617 percentage. By winning 38 of their final 48 games, a fantastic pace, the Mets ended up with more victories than any other major-league team except the Baltimore Orioles.

The Mets had practically a full roster of genuine heroes. Ken Boswell, the second baseman with the cold hands, swung a hot bat the last six weeks of the season and lifted his batting average more than thirty points. Jerry Grote, the catcher, played the final two months of the season like the All-Star he had been in 1968. Cleon Jones, although he lost his bid to win the National League batting title, finished the year at .340, thirty-four points higher than any Met had ever batted before. Jerry Koosman, after his slow start, wound up the year with seventeen victories. And Tom Seaver, the personification of the Mets, was the only pitcher in baseball who won twenty-five games. He lost only seven and posted an earned run average of 2.21. Art Shamsky, Tommie Agee, Donn Clendenon, Tug McGraw—almost every Met—and, especially, the manager, Gil Hodges, contributed significantly to the team's success.

The Mets were the champions of the East, but still, in order to rule the National League they had to overcome the champions of the West, the Atlanta Braves. The oddsmakers, who had dismissed the Mets on sheer logic in the spring, made the New Yorkers underdogs in the playoff series (even though New York had won eight of twelve regular-season games from the Braves).

Baseball men wisely predicted that the Mets could win the best-three-out-of-five playoff series only if their great pitching —Seaver, Koosman and Gentry—could stifle Atlanta's great hitting, the strong bats of Hank Aaron, Orlando Cepeda, and Rico Carty.

The Met's pitching collapsed in the playoffs.

In the first game, Tom Seaver lasted only seven innings and surrendered five runs.

In the second game, Jerry Koosman lasted less than five innings and surrendered six runs.

In the third game, Gary Gentry lasted only two innings and surrendered two runs.

Hank Aaron hit a home run each game. Orlando Cepeda had five hits in the three games. Rico Carty had a hit every game.

And the Mets won all three playoff games.

The details defy belief:

In the first game, the Mets pounded out ten hits, including three by Art Shamsky, rallied for five runs in the eighth inning, and beat the Braves, 9–5.

In the second game, the Mets pounded out thirteen hits, including three more by Shamsky and three by Cleon Jones and home runs by Jones, Tommie Agee, and Ken Boswell, and beat the Braves, 11–6.

In the third game, the Mets pounded out fourteen hits, including three by Boswell and three by Agee and home runs by Agee, Boswell (who had hit only three all season), and Wayne Garrett (who had hit only one all season, way back in the first week of May), and beat the Braves, 7–4.

The Mets pitching staff, which had permitted opponents only 2.99 earned runs a game during the regular season, gave up fully 5.00 earned runs per playoff game.

But the Mets hitters, who had compiled a team batting aver-

218

age of merely .243 during the regular season, batted .327 in the playoff series.

Once again, the champagne flowed in the locker room at Shea Stadium. And once again, the Mets were considered underdogs, this time the champions of the American League, the Baltimore Orioles, who had won their playoff series in three straight games from the Minnesota Twins—the Baltimore Orioles of Frank Robinson, Brooks Robinson, and Boog Powell.

The World Series shaped up as the Miracle vs. the Machine, and, in this mechanized age, few people thought the Mets had a chance. One Baltimore sportswriter, on the eve of the World Series, wrote an essay about reality. The Mets were going to discover reality, he suggested; their impossible dream was about to end.

And, in the first game, in Baltimore, reality triumphed. Mike Cuellar of the Orioles outpitched Tom Seaver, and the Orioles won, 4–1. The first Baltimore batter, Don Buford, hit a home run, and the Mets could work none of their magic. The baseball experts, in all their wisdom, promptly hailed the Baltimore Orioles as one of the sport's great teams of all time, a remarkably gifted and balanced collection of pitchers, hitters, and fielders.

After the first game, reality took a holiday.

In the second game, Donn Clendenon hit a home run and Jerry Koosman, with relief in the ninth inning from Ron Taylor, beat the Orioles, 2–1.

In the third game, Gary Gentry and Nolan Ryan teamed up to shut out the Orioles, 5–0. Tommie Agee led off the game with a home run, but, more importantly, made two spectacular catches, one with the bases loaded, one with two men on, that saved at least five runs.

In the fourth game, Tom Seaver dueled with Mike Cuellar again, and this time Seaver won. Clendenon's home run was the only run of the game until the ninth inning, but then Seaver, tiring, allowed the Orioles to tie the score. Only a running, diving catch by Ron Swoboda in right field prevented the Orioles from scoring again in the ninth inning. In the tenth inning, naturally, just as if it had been scripted, the Mets won the game, 2–1, on a double, an intentional walk, and a misplayed bunt.

Reality was finished.

The fifth game, like the third and fourth, was played at

Shea Stadium, and the Mets, who had won both the Eastern Division and National League titles on their home field, wanted to entertain the New York fans once more. But the Orioles got off to a quick start and took a 3–0 lead. It seemed likely that the World Series would return to Baltimore.

Then, in the bottom of the sixth inning, a pitch nicked Cleon Jones' foot, and the next batter, Donn Clendenon, powered his third home run of the World Series. The Mets moved up to 3–2.

In the bottom of the seventh inning, skinny Al Weis came up to bat for the Mets. He had finished the regular season with a total of two home runs, and two he had hit in Chicago on consecutive days, July 15 and July 16. Now, leading off, he hit another home run, over the fence 371 feet deep in left-center field, and the Mets were even, 3–3.

The rest was anticlimactic. In the bottom of the eighth inning, Cleon Jones led off with a double, and the Mets came up with two runs. Jerry Koosman wrapped up his second World Series victory; New York won, 5–3; the champagne cases came out.

The Mets were the champions of the whole world.

Donn Clendenon, who had joined the Mets in July, discarded by the Montreal Expos, was named the most valuable player in the World Series.

Al Weis, the substitute, was the leading hitter in the World Series with an average of .454, more than double what he batted during the regular season.

Gil Hodges was the manager of the year, the decade, perhaps the century.

The Mets were the champions of the whole world.

Whatever happened to Marvelous Marv?

FINAL STANDINGS
NATIONAL LEAGUE
EASTERN DIVISION

	W	L	PCT.	G.B.
NEW YORK	100	62	.617	–
CHICAGO	92	70	.568	8
PITTSBURGH	88	74	.543	12
ST. LOUIS	87	75	.537	13
PHILADELPHIA	63	99	.389	37
MONTREAL	52	110	.321	48

FINAL 1969 MET STATISTICS

PITCHERS	WON	LOST	E.R.A.
Tom Seaver	25	7	2.21
Jerry Koosman	17	9	2.28
Gary Gentry	13	12	3.42
Tug McGraw	9	3	2.25
Ron Taylor	9	4	2.72
Don Cardwell	8	10	3.02
Nolan Ryan	6	3	3.54
Cal Koonce	6	3	4.99
Jim McAndrew	6	7	3.47
Jack DiLauro	1	4	2.39

HITTERS	HR	RBI	B.A.
Cleon Jones	12	75	.340
Art Shamsky	14	47	.300
Ken Boswell	3	32	.279
Tommie Agee	26	76	.271
Duffy Dyer	3	12	.257
Jerry Grote	6	40	.252
Donn Clendenon	16	51	.248
Bud Harrelson	0	24	.248
Ed Kranepool	11	49	.238
Ron Swoboda	9	52	.235
Bobby Pfeil	0	10	.232
Rod Gaspar	1	14	.228
Wayne Garrett	1	39	.218
Al Weis	2	23	.215
J. C. Martin	4	21	.209
Ed Charles	3	18	.207

NEW YORK METS
POST-SEASON GAMES

NATIONAL LEAGUE PLAYOFF

New York 9, Atlanta 5
New York 11, Atlanta 6
New York 7, Atlanta 4

WORLD SERIES

Baltimore 4, New York 1
New York 2, Baltimore 1
New York 5, Baltimore 0
New York 2, Baltimore 1
New York 5, Baltimore 3

Some SIGNET Biographies You Will Enjoy

☐ **DRAT! W. C. Fields' Picture Book. Edited by Richard J. Anobile—Introduction by Ed McMahon.** DRAT is the encapsulate view, and what a view! of the greatest comedian of the century. Here, in happy juxtaposition of photos and quotes is the irreverent irrelevancy of W. C. Fields, the man and the actor. (#Q3933—95¢)

☐ **MR. LAUREL AND MR. HARDY by John McCabe.** "An affectionate and perceptive dual profile," said **The New York Times** of this biography of two of the greatest comedians of all time. Abundantly illustrated with photographs. With a special foreword by comedian Dick Van Dyke. (#Q3366—95¢)

☐ **THE LONG JOURNEY: A BIOGRAPHY OF SIDNEY POITIER by Carolyn Ewers.** You're handsome, talented, wealthy, adored by millions of women—and you're black. You're the Academy Award winning star of **Lillies of the Field, To Sir, with Love, Guess Who's Coming to Dinner, For Love of Ivy** and **In the Heat of the Night.** (#P3790—60¢)

☐ **BOGIE by Joe Hyams.** The biography of Humphrey Bogart, a great star in his lifetime and now a cult hero for a whole generation who never saw his films while he was alive, written by a close friend of the star, with the authorization and cooperation of Bogart's widow. Introduction by Lauren Bacall. Thirty-two pages of photographs. (#T3071—75¢)